The Poetical Works Of Henry Howard, Earl Of Surrey

BOSTON.
LITTLE BROWN AND

NEW YORK: EVANS AND DICKERSON.
PHILADELPHIA: LIPPINCOTT, GRAMBO AND CO.
M.DCCC.LIV.

THE

POETICAL WORKS

OF

HENRY HOWARD

EARL OF SURREY.

WITH A MEMOIR.

BOSTON:

LITTLE, BROWN AND COMPANY.

NEW YORK: EVANS AND DICKERSON.

PHILADELPHIA: LIPPINCOTT, GRAMBO AND CO.

M.DCCC.LIV.

CAMBRIDGE:

PRINTED BY ALLEN AND FARNHAM.

STEREOTYPED BY STONE AND SMART.

CONTENTS.

	Page
MEMOIR	. vii

SONGS AND SONNETS.

Description of the restless State of a Lover, with Suit to his Lady, to rue on his dying Heart	1
Description of Spring, wherein every thing renews, save only the Lover	3
Description of the restless State of a Lover	4
Description of the fickle Affections, Pangs, and Slights of Love	5
Complaint of a Lover that defied Love, and was by Love after the more tormented	8
Complaint of a Lover rebuked	11
Complaint of the Lover disdained	12
Description and Praise of his Love Geraldine . . .	12
The Frailty and Hurtfulness of Beauty	13
A Complaint by Night of the Lover not beloved . . .	14
How each thing, save the Lover in Spring, reviveth to Pleasure	14
A Vow to love faithfully, howsoever he be rewarded . .	15
Complaint that his Lady, after she knew his Love, kept her Face always hidden from him	16
Request to his Love to join Bounty with Beauty . . .	16
Prisoned in Windsor, he recounteth his Pleasure there passed	17
The Lover comforteth himself with the Worthiness of his Love	20
Complaint of the Absence of her Lover being upon the Sea .	21

Complaint of a dying Lover refused upon his Lady's unjust
    mistaking of his Writing   23
Complaint of the Absence of her Lover, being upon the Sea   27
A Praise of his Love, wherein he reproveth them that com-
    pare their Ladies with his   30
To his Mistress   32
To the Lady that scorned her Lover   32
A Warning to the Lover, how he is abused by his Love   .   34
The forsaken Lover describeth and forsaketh Love   .   .   35
The Lover describeth his restless State   .   .   .   37
The Lover excuseth himself of suspected Change   .   .   39
A careless Man scorning and describing the subtle Usage
    of Women toward their Lovers   41
An Answer in the behalf of a Woman.   Of an uncertain
    Author   43
The constant Lover lamenteth   46
A Song written by the Earl of Surrey of a Lady that refused
    to dance with him   47
The faithful Lover declareth his Pains and his uncertain
    Joys, and with only Hope recomforteth somewhat his
    woful Heart   53
The Means to attain happy Life   57
Praise of mean and constant Estate   58
Praise of certain Psalms of David.   Translated by Sir
    Thomas [Wyatt] the elder.   59
Of the Death of Sir Thomas Wyatt   59
Of the Same   60
Of the Same   62
An Epitaph on Clere, Surrey's faithful Friend and Follower   62
On Sardanapalus's dishonourable Life and miserable Death   64
How no Age is content with his own Estate, and how the
    Age of Children is the happiest if they had Skill to under-
    stand it   65
Bonum est mihi quod humiliasti me   67
Exhortation to learn by others' Trouble   .   .   .   68
The Fancy of a wearier Lover   68
A Satire against the Citizens of London   .   .   .   69
A description of the restless State of the Lover when absent
    from the Mistress of his Heart   71

ECCLESIASTES.

Chapter I. 82
   II. 84
   III. 89
   IV. 93
   V. 96

A PARAPHRASE OF SOME OF THE PSALMS OF DAVID.

Proem 101
Psalm LXXXVIII. 101
  LXXIII. 104
  "Though, Lord, to Israel" 105
  LV. 109
  VIII. 111

The Second Book of Virgil's Æneid 115
The Fourth Book of Virgil's Æneid 153

" My fearful hope from me is fled " 186
" Your fearful hope cannot prevail " · . . . 187

MEMOIR OF HENRY HOWARD EARL OF SURREY.

"I write of him whose fame for aye endures."
Tubervile's Epitaph on Surrey.

DISTINGUISHED alike by his talents and rank, HENRY HOWARD EARL OF SURREY has attracted considerable attention; and as the first writer who attempted to refine our language, and to rescue English poetry from the grossness for which the productions of his predecessors are remarkable, he is worthy of the extraordinary research which his latest biographer has displayed in collecting particulars respecting his history. Dr. Nott affords a very creditable example of industry, and it is no slight praise to say that he appears to have exhausted every available source of information; hence, until a change takes place in the present disgraceful state of the public muniments, it is in vain to hope that any new light can be thrown on the life of this eminent person. The following Memoir has, therefore, been drawn up almost entirely from material

collected by Dr. Nott, an admission which it would
be disingenuous to withhold; but considerable difference will be found with respect to the inferences
which that writer has drawn from some of the facts
he has brought to light; and it is from this circumstance that these sheets derive their claim to attention. The most interesting of the letters which
occur in the appendix to Dr. Nott's edition are here
introduced into the Memoir, and though the present
narrative is destitute of those pleasing speculations
which distinguish that biographer's Life of Surrey,
the loss may, perhaps, be borne with, when it is
remembered that it is as dangerous for a biographer as for an historian to indulge his *imaginative*
powers.

Although the Earl of Surrey owes but little of
the respect which is felt for his memory to the
adventitious splendour of his birth, it is necessary
to speak of his genealogy with some minuteness,
because it was from circumstances arising out of his
pedigree that he became one of the victims of Henry
the Eighth.

Doubts have been expressed as to the remote
antiquity of the family of Howard, but it is beyond
dispute that they descend from Sir William Howard, the Chief Justice of the Common Pleas in the
reigns of Edward the First and Second, whose son,
Sir John, was a Knight Banneret as early as 1307.
His great great-grandson, Sir Robert Howard, married Margaret Mowbray, daughter of Thomas, Duke

of Norfolk and Earl Marshal, whose mother was
Elizabeth, daughter and heiress of John Lord Se-
grave the granddaughter and heiress of Thomas de
Brotherton, Earl of Norfolk, a younger son of King
Edward the First. Sir John Howard, K. G. the
eldest son of Sir Robert by the Lady Margaret
Mowbray, was created a Baron in 1470; and on
the extinction of the Mowbrays, Dukes of Norfolk,
about the year 1480, he became, in right of his
mother, the eldest coheir of that house, which entitled him to quarter whatever arms were borne by
them, a fact, as will afterwards appear, of some importance. Sir John Howard was raised to the duke-
dom of Norfolk by Richard the Third, who at the
same time created his eldest son, Thomas, Earl of
Surrey. These titles were forfeited after the battle
of Bosworth, in which the "Jocky of Norfolk" gallantly fell in the cause of his sovereign and ben-
efactor.

Thomas Howard, his son, was restored to the
earldom of Surrey in 1489; and in reward of his
services at Flodden Field he was created Duke of
Norfolk in February, 1514. Dying in 1524, he
was succeeded by his son Thomas, third Duke of
Norfolk, who was twice married — first to Anne,
daughter of King Edward the Fourth, by whom he
had no issue that survived their childhood, and
secondly to Elizabeth Stafford, daughter of Edward,
Duke of Buckingham, by whom he was father of
the Poet. His second marriage, which proved an

unhappy one, took place about Easter in 1513; the
Duchess was twenty years younger than her husband, and was then the object of an attachment,
which was reciprocal, to the Earl of Westmoreland.

The exact date of the birth of the Earl of Surrey
has not been ascertained, but it may be assigned to
some time between 1516 and 1518; nor has it been
determined where it occurred, though many circumstances render it probable that it took place at
Framlingham in Suffolk.

It would be idle to follow the most elaborate of
Surrey's biographers in his speculations on the
Earl's education, for nothing positive is known of
him, until his fifteenth year, excepting that he was
cupbearer to the King in 1526, and that in July,
1529, he accompanied his father on a visit to the
Prior of Butley, in Suffolk. Early in 1532 he
married Frances Vere, daughter of John, fifteenth
Earl of Oxford, the settlement being dated on the
13th of February, in that year, at which time he
could not have been more than sixteen. According
to several writers Surrey and the Duke of Richmond, the natural son of Henry the Eighth, visited
Paris together in that year, and joined the King in
October, on his Majesty's landing at Calais, whilst
others, with more reason, consider that they left
England as part of the King's retinue. In the account of the ceremonials which occurred at the in-
terview between Henry and the King of France, at
Boulogne on this occasion, the Duke of Richmond

and the Earl of Surrey are mentioned as having been present. Richmond went to Paris to complete his studies, and it is supposed that Surrey accompanied him, but his stay could not have been of long duration, for at the coronation of Anne Boleyn, in June, 1533, he bore one of the swords which were carried in the procession. Richmond, who returned to England with the Duke of Norfolk in the autumn of that year, was, in September, affianced to Lady Mary Howard, Surrey's only sister, but as the parties were related within the fourth degrees of consanguinity, a dispensation was necessary. The young Duke was placed at Windsor, whilst his bride continued to live with her father, and it was at this time, and not, as had been previously supposed, in his childhood,* that Surrey was the companion of Richmond at Windsor. Speaking of this period of his life, Surrey says,

> "—— proud Windsor, where I in lust and joy,
> With a Kinges son, my childish years did pass,
> In greater feast than Priam's sons of Troy.
> Where each sweet place returns a taste full sour.
> The large green courts, where we were wont to hove,
> With eyes cast up into the Maiden's tower,
> And easy sighs, such as folk draw in love.
> The stately seats, the ladies bright of hue.
> The dances short, long tales of great delight;
> With words and looks, that tigers could but rue;
> Where each of us did plead the other's right.
> The palme-play, where, despoiled for the game,
> With dazed eyes oft we by gleams of love

---

* Nott's Life of Surrey.

> Have miss'd the ball, and got sight of our dame,
> To bait her eyes, which kept the leads above.
> The gravel'd ground, with sleeves tied on the helm,
> On foaming horse, with swords and friendly hearts;
> With chere, as though one should another whelm,
> Where we have fought, and chased oft with darts.
> With silver drops the mead yet spread for ruth,
> In active games of nimbleness and strength,
> Where we did strain, trained with swarms of youth,
> Our tender limbs, that yet shot up in length.
> The secret groves which oft we made resound
> Of pleasant plaint and of our ladies' praise;
> Recording soft what grace each one had found,
> What hope of speed, what dread of long delays."

These "delays," so far as Surrey was concerned, could not have exceeded two years; for on the 10th of March, 1536, his eldest son was born. On the 18th of October following, he received the honour of Knighthood, and he soon afterwards took a conspicuous part in public affairs. At the trial of his kinswoman, the unfortunate Anne Boleyn, he was present as the representative of the Earl Marshal, his father having presided by virtue of his office of Lord Treasurer. Within a few months of her execution the tyrannical disposition of Henry the Eighth was manifested towards Surrey's uncle, Lord Thomas Howard, who was committed to the Tower for having married the Lady Margaret Douglas without the King's permission. After being confined for two years he died of a broken heart, an event which made a deep impression upon the poet, and he adverts to it in one of his poems: —

————————— " It is not long ago,
Sith that for love one of the race did end his life in woe,
In tower both strong and high, for his assured truth,
Whereas in tears he spent his breath, alas! the more tho
    ruth.
This gentle breast so died, whom nothing could remove,
But willingly to lese his life for loss of his true love."

But he experienced a heavier calamity in the
same year by the death of his friend and brother-in-
law the Duke of Richmond, of whom he speaks with
the greatest affection in a poem written some time
after his decease.*

It is here necessary to advert to Surrey's suppos-
ititious passion for the fair Geraldine, a circumstance
which has imparted a romantic interest to his life,
but which, like most romantic stories, is without any
solid foundation. Many of his biographers have
considered that the lady thus designated was the
object of a real attachment, and so strongly was Dr.
Nott impressed with this opinion, that he has ven-
tured to place an address to Geraldine as the title
of nearly all the Earl's sonnets, not only without
any authority, but in contradiction to the first, and,
it is believed, every other edition of his works.
This gratuitous assumption has led that writer into
serious errors: he has deemed many lines in various
poems to be illustrative of the history of Surrey's
passion for Geraldine, which evidently refer to a
different person; and several pages occur on the

* See page 19.

subject, upon which all that is necessary to be said is, that they indicate a very fertile imagination.*

One poem, and one poem *only* can, upon any thing like evidence, be supposed to have been addressed to the lady mentioned by the name of Geraldine, and there is every reason to adopt Horace Walpole's opinion, that she was Elizabeth, the daughter of Gerald Fitz-Gerald, ninth Earl of Kildare; but, unless it is to be assumed that all verses which celebrate a lady's beauty arise from a real instead of an imaginary passion, it is impossible to believe that Surrey was seriously in love with the fair Geraldine. The person alluded to was a mere child, not more than thirteen years old. Surrey was then married, and, for aught that appears to the contrary, was living happily with his wife, whose birth was equal to his own. His attachment, if it really existed, for Geraldine must, therefore, have been an illicit one; and it betrays little sagacity to suppose that a young married nobleman would have publicly avowed a passion for the daughter of a powerful earl, connected with the highest families in the realm, and who was then living under the especial protection of her cousin the Princess Mary.†

* See Nott's Life of Surrey, pages cxxi. to cxxvii.
† Dr. Nott's account of Geraldine is as follows: —
"She was the daughter to Gerald Fitz-Gerald, ninth Earl of Kildare, whose ancestors were supposed to have descended from the Geraldi of Florence. Her mother was daughter to Thomas Marquis of Dorset. She was born in Ireland, probably at the

So absurd is the opinion which has hitherto prevailed upon this subject, that no further notice will
be taken of it, than to point out what appear to be
the facts of the case. Surrey seems to have met
the Lady Elizabeth Fitz Gerald at Hunsdon, the
residence of the Princess Mary, and he again saw
her at Hampton Court, when he was so much pleased
with her as to be induced to celebrate her virtues
and budding charms in a sonnet. Availing himself
of the license allowed to poets of all periods, he
addressed her as the object of his affections, and
from the line in which he says that Windsor then

Castle of Maynooth, her father's principal place of residence,
about the year 1528; and was brought into England whilst yet
an infant.

" The subsequent misfortunes of her family, in 1533, rendered
her an object of pity to Henry, to whom she was nearly related
by birth. Whether the protection afforded by Henry to the fair
Geraldine was an act of spontaneous kindness on his part, or one
granted at the solicitation of her mother, the Countess, is not
known. It is certain that, when a child, she was educated in the
house of the Lady Mary, not as the companion of that Princess's
studies, for the Princess Mary must have been fourteen years
old when the fair Geraldine was born, but from motives of pity
and benevolence.

" When she had grown up to be of a sufficient age to attend
upon the Lady Mary, she became one of her ladies of the chamber. This probably was about the year 1542, when the fair
Geraldine must have been about fourteen.

" Some time in the year 1543 she married to Sir Anthony
Brown. She could not then have been much more than fifteen
years old. Sir Anthony Brown must have been sixty. After
his death, which happened in 1449, she became the third wife
of Henry Clinton, Earl of Lincoln, whom she survived."

concealed her from his sight, it may be inferred that
the poem was written either during his residence at
Windsor, or when she was there and he elsewhere.

It is remarkable that whilst so extravagant a de-
duction has been drawn from one solitary sonnet,
no notice has been hitherto taken of a poem which
bears striking marks of being dictated by the affection which subsisted between him and his Countess.*

At the funeral of Queen Jane Seymour, in October, 1537, Surrey attended as one of the principal
mourners: he was present at Court on New Year's
Day following, and presented the King with three
gilt bowls. In the spring of 1539 his second son,
Henry, who was afterwards created Earl of Northampton, was born.

Surrey particularly distinguished himself at the
jousts and tournaments which were held in honour
of the King's marriage with Anne of Cleves, in
1540, and towards the close of that year he accompanied the forces which were sent to put Guisnes
into a state of defence, in case of a rupture with
France, when he commenced his military career;
his stay there was however very short; and in September, in the same year, he and his father were
appointed stewards of the University of Cambridge.

Early in 1541 Sir Edmund Knyvett struck the
Earl's friend and attendant, Thomas Clere, within
the precincts of the Court. For this offence the
usual punishment of the loss of the right hand was

* See pp. 27–30.

pronounced, but at Surrey's intercession, says Dr.
Nott, Knyvett was pardoned. The authority for
attributing his escape to him is not mentioned, and
the assertion is contradicted by a passage in Holling-
shed, whence it seems that the penalty was remitted
in consequence of an appeal to the King's generosity
from the culprit himself.

On St. George's Day, 1542, Surrey received one
of the highest favours which his sovereign could con-
fer, by being elected a Knight of the Garter. A
few months afterwards he was involved in a quarrel
with a gentleman of the name of John a Leigh,
whom he challenged, and the dispute has, without a
shadow of proof, been attributed to Leigh's being
his rival in Geraldine's affections! * Be the cause
however what it might, Surrey was evidently in fault,
for he was sent a prisoner to the Fleet, being allowed two servants to attend upon him, but none
was permitted to banquet with him. The first of
Surrey's letters which has been discovered was written whilst he was in confinement, and is of much interest. It was addressed to the Privy Council, and
entreated them to obtain his liberation, or at least to
intercede that he might be removed to a less "noisome" prison : —

"MY VERY GOOD LORDS,

"AFTER my humble commendations to your Lordships; these presents shall be to advertise you, that

* Nott, page 1.

B

albeit I have of late severally required each of you,
by my servant Pickering, of your favour; from
whom as yet I have received no other comfort
than my passed folly hath deserved; I have yet
thought it my duty again, as well to renew my suit,
as humbly to require you rather to impute this error
to the fury of reckless youth, than to a will not
comformable and contented, with the quiet learning
of the just reward of my folly; for as much as I so
suddenly and quickly did procure and attempt to
seek for friendship, and intreat for my deliverance:
as then not sufficiently pondering nor debating with
myself, that a prince offended hath none redress
upon his subject but condign punishment, without
respect of person. Yet, let my youth unpractised
in durance obtain pardon: (although for lack of
strength it yield not itself wholly to his gentle chastisement,) whilst the heart is resolved in patience
to pass over the same, in satisfaction of mine errors.

" And, my Lords, if it were lawful to persuade by
the precedent of other young men reconciled, I
would affirm that this might sound to me a happy
fault: by so gentle a warning to learn how to bridle
my heady will: which in youth is rarely attained
without adversity. Where, might I without vaunt
lay before you the quiet conversation of my passed
life; which (unstained with any unhonest touch,
unseeming in such a man as it hath pleased God
and the King to make me), might perfectly promise
new amendment of mine offence. Whereof, if you

doubt in any point, I shall humbly desire you, that during mine affliction, (in which time malice is most ready to slander the innocent,) there may be made an whole examination of my life: wishing, for the better trial thereof, to have the time of my durance redoubled; and so (declared as well tried, and unsuspected) by your mediations to be restored to the King's favour; than, condemned in your grave heads, without answer or further examination to be quickly delivered: this heinous offence always unexcused, whereupon I was committed to this noisome prison; whose pestilent airs are not unlike to bring some alteration of health.

"Wherefore, if your good Lordships judge me not a member rather to be clean cut away, than reformed; it may please you to be suitors to the King's Majesty on my behalf; as well for his favour, as for my liberty: or else, at the least, if his pleasure be to punish this oversight with the forbearing his presence; (which unto every loving subject, specially unto me, from a Prince cannot be less counted than a living death,) yet it would please him to command me into the country, to some place of open air, with like restraint of liberty, there to abide his Grace's pleasure.

"Finally, albeit no part of this my trespass in any way to do me good, I should judge me happy if it should please the King's Majesty to think, that this simple body rashly adventured in the revenge of his own quarrel, shall be without respect always ready to be employed in his service; trusting once so to redouble this error, which may be well repeated but not revoked. Desiring your good Lordships that like as my offence hath not been, my submission may likewise appear: which is all the recompense that I may well think my doings answer not. Your grave heads should yet consider, that neither am I the first young man that hath enterprised such things as he hath afterward repented."

He continued a prisoner until the 7th of August, when he was released upon his recognizance in ten thousand marks not to offer any further offence, by word or deed, to Leigh or to any of his friends. War being soon afterwards declared against Scotland, Lord Surrey accompanied the expedition into that kingdom, under his father the Duke of Norfolk, but it is not known what rank he bore in the army. It is evident, from his epitaph on his friend Clere, that he was present at the burning of Kelsal; but on breaking up the English forces soon afterwards, the Earl returned to London.

An affair occurred within a few months which is remarkable for two reasons, the one as proving that Surrey was of an intemperate, and if the previous dispute with Leigh be remembered, perhaps quarrelsome and impetuous temper; the other for its affording a memorable instance of the facility with which a biographer can make any fact redound to the honour of his hero. On the 1st of April, 1543, the Earl was summoned before the Privy Council, and

charged with two offences, having eaten flesh in
Lent, and having walked about the streets of the
city at night in a "lewd and unseemly manner," and
breaking several windows with a stone-bow. To the
first charge he replied, that he had a license; but to
the latter he pleaded guilty, and submitted himself to
such punishment as might be thought proper, whereupon he was again sent to the Fleet.* In this
midnight affair of breaking windows, it is difficult to
recognize any other conduct than what now, as then,
is often produced by wine in young men bent on
mischief, who disguise the impropriety of their
actions under the names of fun and frolic. Dr.
Nott however describes his behaviour as "interesting," because it "marks the romantic turn of his
mind, and enables us to form some opinion as to the
nature of his sentiments on the subject of religion!" †
The ground for this remark is the account which
Surrey gives of the transaction in the poem entitled

* "At St. James's, the 1st day of April, 1543. The Earl of
Surrey being sent for to appear before the Council, was charged
by the said presence as well of eating flesh, as of a lewd and
unseemly manner of walking in the night about the streets, and
breaking with stone-bows of certain windows. And touching
the eating of flesh, he alleged a license; albeit he had not so
secretly used the same as appertained: and touching the stone-
bows, he could not deny but he had very evil doings therein,
submitting himself, therefore, to such punishment as should to
them be thought good; whereupon he was committed to the
Fleet." — *Privy Council Book of the reign of Henry VIII.*

† Nott's Memoirs of Surrey, page lii.

"a Satire against the Citizens of London," * in
which he says he endeavoured to awaken them to
a sense of their iniquities by flinging stones against
their windows. This satirical piece has been grave-
ly paraphrased, as if it were the argument which
the Earl used to the Privy Council, and comments
are made upon it to explain why his virtuous motive
was not allowed to extenuate so flagrant a breach
of the peace ! †

The simple explanation of that poem is that,
when in confinement, Surrey gratified his spleen
against the citizens, whose complaint produced his
imprisonment, by a satirical allusion to their vices,
and he wittily says, that his conduct was intended
as a punishment of their crimes. His companions
in the outrage, Pickering and the young Wyatt,
were both sent to prison,‡ and it would seem that

* See page 69.

† Nott's Memoir, page lii.

‡ "The same day [April the first] were also called Thomas
Wyatt and young Pickering; and being charged with the same
offences, they confessed the first, alleging therefore their [li-
cense]: but in the second, touching the stone-bows, they utterly
stood denial, notwithstanding they were condemned to shew the
truth thereof upon their allegiance : whereupon Wyatt was
commanded to the Counter, and Pickering to the Porter's
Lodge. *Privy Council Books.* The next day they were called
again before the council, and, after some resistance, at last confessed the offence; on which they were committed to the Tower.
They were not liberated till the third of May ensuing, enter-
ing then into a recognisance of 200*l.* each for their good behav-

their religious zeal is deemed by Dr. Nott to have been no less fervent than that of the Earl. So that to break the windows of Catholics, when peaceably asleep in their beds, is evidence that the offender was no papist; that though this was a "wild and extravagant attempt at reformation, it is certain that it was the result of sincerity on the part of Surrey, and grew out of that romantic turn of thought and enthusiastic mode of contemplating common objects which was peculiar to him!" *

Surrey's imprisonment was probably of short duration; and in October following, his father sent him to Sir John Wallop, the commander of the army with which Henry had assisted the Emperor. He joined the allied camp before Landrecy, near Boulogne, being attended by his faithful servants Clere and Blage. Wallop thus announced his arrival to the King: —

"Yesterday Blage, who arrived here with my Lord of Surrey, went with Mr. Carew to see the trench, and escaped very hardly from a piece of ordnance that was shot towards him. My said Lord I brought about a great part of the town to view the same; and in his return was somewhat saluted. Their powder and shot they do bestow amongst us plentifully, and sometime doth hurt. My said Lord's coming unto this camp was very agreeable

iour. *Ibid.* 89. No notice is taken of the time of Surrey's liberation." — *Nott's Memoir.*

* Nott, page liv.

unto the Duke, and great Master, declaring a great amity and friendship that your Majesty beareth to the Emperor. I was very glad that my said Lord intended to go unto Fernando's camp, informing him, as they offered him sufficient conduct, and the great Master himself to bring him half way there."

In various letters from Sir John Wallop, Surrey's assiduity in acquiring military knowledge is mentioned in terms of praise; but the operations of the army are too uninteresting to be detailed, and it is sufficient to state, that the Earl returned with it to England in November. It is presumed that he employed himself for some time afterwards in constructing his beautiful seat called Mount Surrey, near Norwich; and about this period he received the celebrated Hadrian Junius into his family as physician, assigning him apartments at Kenninghall, with a yearly salary of fifty angels. Near this time too the poet Churchyard seems to have been one of the Earl's pages, as it appears from some verses in which he paints Surrey's talents and virtues in glowing colours, that he was for four years one of his retainers.*

---

* A master of no mean estate, a mirror in those days,
His happy fortune then him gat, whose virtues must I praise.
More heavenly were those gifts he had than earthly was his
   form,
His corpse too worthy for the grave, his flesh no meat for worm.
An Earl of birth; a God of sprite, a Tully for his tongue;
Methink of right the world should shake when half his praise
   were rung.

Whatever may have been the young Earl's happiness in his own family, the situation of his parents must have occasioned him much uneasiness; and it is to be regretted that his mother should have had to accuse him of unkindness. For several years after their marriage, the Duke and Duchess lived together in comparative harmony, but about 1533, when Surrey was not more than seventeen, a sepa-

Oh! cursed were those crooked crafts, that his own country
   wrought
To chop off such a chosen head as our time ne'er forth brought.
His knowledge crept beyond the stars and wrought to Jove's
   high throne,
The bowels of the earth he saw, in his deep breast y-known.
His wit looked through each man's device; his judgment
   grounded was,
Almost he had foresight to know ere things should come to pass;
When they should fall; what should betide, Oh! what a loss of
   weight
Was it to lose so ripe a head, that reached to such height!
In every heart he feeling had: with pen past Petrarch sure,
A fashion framed which could his foes to friendship oft allure,
His virtues could not keep him here, but rather wrought his
   harms,
And made his enemies murmur oft, and brought them in by
   swarms.
Whose practice put him to his plunge, and lost his life thereby,
O! canker'd breasts which have such hearts wherein such hate
   doth lie.
As I have told this young man served this master twice two
   year,
And learned therein such fruitful skill, as long he held full dear.
And used the pen as he was taught and other gifts also,
Which made him hold the cap on head, where some do crouch
   full low.

ration took place.   From not receiving a proper
allowance for her support, she complained to Cromwell, the Lord Privy Seal, praying him to intercede
on the subject.   As her letters are curious, and
afford some information about Surrey, extracts from
them are desirable illustrations of this Memoir.   The
first of these letters was written at Redborne in
Hertfordshire, in December, 1536.   Alluding to
some proposition which had been made her, she
says : —

"My Lord, since I came home I had a letter
from my aunt Hastings, and she desires me to deny
the said two articles : and I do send to Mr. Richard
Cromwell a copy of the letter of the answer I made
to her, to deliver to you ; which I pray you take the
pains to over-read, at your coming into leisure : and
there you shall perceive that I will never deny the
said two articles during my life.   And so I pray you
shew my Lord my husband, that I will never deny
them, for no ill handling that he can do to me ; nor
for no imprisonment ; so I pray you shew my Lord
my husband that he may trust to it, seeing that I will
not do it at the King's commandment, nor at your
desire.   I will not do it for no friend nor kin I have
living : nor from this day forward I will never sue
to the King, nor to none other, to desire my Lord
my husband to take me again : for I have made
much suit to him and nothing regarded : and I made
him no fault, but in declaring of his shameful handling of me ; as I have written to you my Lord, in

other letters before. There shall no imprisonment
change my mind, nor a less living. I pray you, my
Lord, to be in hand with the King to expedite me
a better living, ere my Lord my husband go northward: for I have but £50 the quarter, and here I
lie in a dear country, and I but three hundred marks
a year. I have been from my husband, come the
Tuesday in the Passion week, three years. Though
I be left poorly, yet I am content withal, for I am
out of danger of mine enemies, and of the ill life
that I had with my Lord my husband since he loved
Bess Holland first, who was but washer of my
nursery eight years, and she hath been the causer
of all my trouble. I pray you, my Lord, when you
be at leisure, write to me an answer whether I shall
have a better living or not: for if my Lord my husband go northward, I will get me into some other
quarter, where I may be better cheap. I am fully
determined never to write nor to send more to my
Lord my husband as long as I live, how poorly
soever I live; for he never sent me answer of the
last letter that I did write to him by the King's
commandment; no, nor answer of the two gentle
letters that I wrote to him before. And if he shall
take me again, I know well it is more for the shame
of the world than for any love he beareth me; for
I know well, my life shall be as ill as ever it was.
I have been well used, since I have been from him,
to a quiet life, and if I should come to him, to use
me as he did, he would grete me worse now than

it did before; because I have lived quiet these three years, without brawling or fighting. I may say I was born in an unhappy hour to be matched with such an ungracious husband, and so ungracious a son and daughter."

In June, 1537, the Duchess requested Lord Cromwell to inform her whether her income was to be increased or not, and begged him to speak to her husband to that purpose. She says : —

" My trust is in you next God. For if the King's Grace granteth my daughter of Richmond her jointure (which he had never penny for at her marriage), I know well, if the King command my husband, that I shall have my whole jointure. If my daughter's jointure be granted before, he will not let me have the remainder of my jointure by the King's commandment; nor at your good Lordship's desire neither, though, my Lord, my father paid two thousand marks with me, with other great charges, as I have written to you before : which my Lord my husband hath forgotten now he hath so much wealth and honours, and is so far in doting love with that queen, that he neither regardeth God nor his honour. He knoweth that it is spoken of far and near, to his great dishonour and shame : and he chose me for love; and I am younger than him by twenty years, and he hath put me away four years and a quarter at this Midsummer. I have lived always like a good woman, as it is not unknown to him. I was daily waiter in the court sixteen years together, when he hath lived from me more than a year in the King's wars. The King's Grace shall be my record how I used myself, without any ill name or fame: and the best in the Court, that were there that time, both men and women, know how I used myself in my younger days: and here is a poor reward I have in my latter days for my well doing! and it is the least I shall have, without your good help, my Lord. He hath taken away all my jewels and my apparel, and left me four years and more like a prisoner, as I have written you before: and none comes at me but such as he appointeth. I have made suit to him three times with three gentle letters. One of them was by the King's commandment, when I was with his Majesty at Dunstable: and I have sent you the copies of them all three. I never sent to him since, nor never will during my life. I am full determined, since I was with the King's Grace and you, that I would never make more suit to nobody during my life. I know, my Lord, my husband's crafty ways of old: that he hath made me many times promises under a colour, which he never performed. I will never make more suit unto him, neither for prisonment, nor less living during my life. And besides that, my daughter of Richmond, and Bess Holland is comen up with her; that harlot, which hath put me at this trouble, and it is eleven years since my Lord my husband first fell in love with her, and yet she is but a churl's daughter, and of no gentle blood : but that my Lord my husband hath set him up for her sake, because he was so nigh akin to my Lord Hussey, that was late made, and died last, and was beheaded; and was the head of that drab, Bess Holland's blood. And he keeps her still in his house : and his children maintain the matter : therefore I will never come at him during my life. Another time he set his women to bind me till blood came out at my finger ends ; and pinnacled me ; and set on my breast till I spit blood; and he never punished them. All this was done for Bess Holland's sake, and he sent me word by Master Cornysh that he would serve me so, two years before he put me away. I know well, if I should come home again, my life should be but short."

Her remonstrances were repeated in November of the same year, but the only passages worthy of notice are, the assertion that the Duke wished to divorce her, and that though her children were unkind to her, she always loved them. In October, 1538, she said to Cromwell,

" I pray you, my Lord, now my Lord my husband is coming home, that you will be in hand with him for a better living, seeing he has away all my jewels and my apparel, and had with me two thousand marks, which is more, by times, than ever. He had but little to take to when he married me first but his lands, and he was always a great player. Seeing my Lord my father made me sure of five hundred marks a year, and seeing that my Lord my

husband chose me himself: for my Lord my father
had chose my Lord of Westmoreland for me; he
and I had loved together two years, and if my
Lord my husband had not sent immediately word
after my lady, and my Lord's first wife was dead,
and made suit to my Lord my father, or else I had
been married before Christmas to my Lord of Westmoreland, and it was my Lord my husband's suit to
my Lord my father, and never came of me nor none
of my friends: and when he came thither at Easter
tide, he would have none of my sisters, but only me.
My Lord, seeing I have been his wife twenty-five
years, and have borne him five children, and can
lay nothing to my charge, but for because I would not
be contented to suffer the harlots that bound me to
be still in the house. They bound me and pinnacled
me, and sat on my breast till I spit blood, which I
have been worse for ever since, and all for speaking
against the woman in the Court, Bess Holland;
therefore he put me out of the doors. Surely, my
Lord, I am full determined that I will never make
suit to him to come in his company whilst I live,
seeing that the King's Grace and you can make no
end. I will never make suit to none creature more,
nor I myself to my Lord my husband, nor I will
never come at him during my life. It is four year
come the Tuesday in the Passion week that he came
riding all night, and locked me up in a chamber,
and took away all my jewels and all my apparel,

and never gave me but fifty pounds a quarter,
which is three hundred marks a year, and therewith I keep twenty persons, and I lie in a hard
county."

Cromwell advised her to return to her husband;
but in a letter dated the 29th January, 1538–9, she
thus declined to comply with his suggestions : —

"I pray you, my Lord, to take no displeasure
that I do not follow your counsel to go home to my
Lord my husband again, which I will never do during my life, neither for imprisonment, nor for less
living, which I have been threatened often enough,
since I was with the King's Grace at Dunstable,
three years and a half ago, and put my matter to
his Grace to make an end, and to your Lordship;
then my Lord my husband refused it. I then made
promise that I would never sue to come to him
again during my life. It is six years come Easter,
that my Lord my husband put me away; and your
Lordship knoweth that I have submitted myself in
three letters, which your Lordship have seen, and
in this three years he never sent to me gentle message, but always cruel messages and threatenings;
and he keepeth that harlot Bess Holland, and all
the residue of the harlots that bound me, and pinnacled me, and sat on my breast till they made me
spit blood, and I have been the worse ever since;
and I reckon that if I should come home again I
should be poisoned for the love that he beareth to

the harlot Bess Holland, and he would as well hold
them in that as he did the residue which bound me;
as I have rehearsed before. I will never never
come at my Lord my husband for no fair promises
nor cruel handling. I had rather be kept in the
Tower of London during my life, for I am so well
used to imprisonment I care not for it; for he will
suffer no gentlemen to come at me, but Master
Cornish and Master Roylet, and very few gentle-
women.

"I beseech you to have pity upon me, and remember I am a gentlewoman born, and hath been
brought up decently, and not to live so barely as
I do, with £50 a quarter, and the one quarter, and
half the other quarter is spent before it cometh in;
and besides, I am visited much with sickness, and
specially now a late, and many times besides since
I came to Redburne; and now age cometh on apace
with me; and besides that, there was never woman
that bare so ungracious an eldest son, and so ungracious a daughter, and unnatural, as I have done."

The last letter on this painful subject is from the
Duke of Norfolk, which is likewise addressed to
Lord Cromwell, and as it presents another picture
of the dispute, it will be given at length:—

"MY VERY GOOD LORD,

"It is come to my knowledge that my wilful wife
is come to London, and hath be with you yester-

night to come to me to London.   My Lord, I assure
you as long as I live I will never come in her company, unto the time she hath first written to me that
she hath untruly slandered me in writing and saying, that when she had been in childbed of my
daughter of Richmond two nights and a day, I
should draw her out of her bed by the hair of her
head, about the house, and with my dagger give her
a wound in her head.

"My good Lord, if I prove not by witness, and
that with many honest persons, that she had the
scar in her head fifteen months before she was
delivered of my said daughter, and that the same
was cut by a surgeon of London, for a swelling she
had in her head, of drawing two teeth, never trust
my word after: reporting to your good Lordship
whether I shall play the felo or no, to put me in
her danger, that so falsely will slander me, and so
wilfully stick thereby.   Surely I think there is no
man on live that would handle a woman in childbed of that sort, nor for my part would no so have
done for all that I am worth.

"Finally, my Lord, I require you to send to her
in no wise to come where I am, for the same shall
not only put me to more trouble than I have (whereof I have no need), but might give me occasion to
handle her otherwise than I have done yet.   If she
first write to me, confessing her false slander, and
thereupon sue to the King's highness to make any

deed, I will never refuse so do that his majesty shall command me to do; but before, assuredly never. And thus heartily fare ye well.

"From Bontyngfere, this Friday before day,

"Your own assuredly,

"T. NORFOLK."

It would be vain to inquire how far the Duchess was the injured party; but it is remarkable if she were ill treated by her husband that her children should all have taken part with their father.

About July, 1544, Henry again invaded France with a large army, the vanguard of which was commanded by the Duke of Norfolk, and Surrey was appointed Marshal, an office of considerable importance, and requiring capacity and courage. The van and rearguard having joined the Emperor's forces, they laid siege to Montreuil, and on the 26th of July Henry invested Boulogne in person. As that town was the principal object of the King's attention all the resources were bestowed upon the besiegers, and his troops before Montreuil were allowed to want ammunition and pay. Norfolk's exertions did not, however, relax; and, aided by his son, he succeeded in distressing the garrison by famine. Surrey more than once distinguished himself during the siege, and his services are thus mentioned in one of his father's despatches: —

"With hearty recommendations this shall be to advertise your good Lordships that this evening

Monsieur de Bewers with his band, and my son of
Surrey, my Lord of Sussex, my Lord Mountjoy, my
brother William, my Lord Latimer, Mr. Treasurer,
and all the rest of the noblemen whom I sent further
upon Saturday at ten at night, returned hither to
this camp this night at seven o'clock, without loss
of any man slain, and have made a very honest
journey, and have burnt the towns of Saint Riquier
and Riew, both walled towns, and also the fauxbourg
of Abbeville, on this side of the town, where the
English horsemen had a right hot skirmish, and
after the coming of the whole army retired without
loss, and burned all the country; and they of Crotey
fearing our men would have laid siege to the castle,
burned their own town. Our men have brought a
very great booty of all sorts of cattle; the noblemen
and gentlemen kept their footmen in such order,
that they borrowed nothing of the Burgonians, and
finally have made such an excourse, that the like
hath not been made since these wars began."

In an attempt to storm Montreuil on the 19th of
September, the Earl was either wounded or much
exhausted, and he owed his life to the fidelity of
Clere, who in bringing him off received a hurt which
eventually caused his death. This affecting incident
Surrey has himself commemorated in his epitaph on
Clere : —

> " Tracing whose steps thou sawest Kelsal blaze,
>   Landrecy burnt, and batter'd Boulogne render.
>   At Montreuil gates, hopeless of all recure,

Thine Earl, half dead, gave in thy hand his will;
Which cause did thee this pining death procure."*

On the 25th of September a reinforcement was
sent to the Duke of Norfolk, but it arrived too late:
the siege of Montreuil was raised, and the English
army retired to Boulogne on the 30th of that month.
Norfolk reached England about the middle of December, and as nothing further is recorded of Surrey until Christmas Day, when he attended a Chapter of the Garter at Hampton Court, it may be
inferred that he came back with his father.   According to Monsieur Du Bellay, Surrey was again at
Boulogne soon afterwards, but this statement is
doubtful, and it is certain that he was present at a
Chapter of the Garter on St. George's Day in 1545.

In July following he was at Kenninghall, in Norfolk, where he received a letter from the Privy
Council respecting some men that were raised for
the expedition for the defence of Boulogne, which was
then menaced by the French.   The Earl was appointed commander of the vanguard, consisting of
five thousand soldiers, with which he arrived at
Calais in August, where he was joined by three
thousand.   On the 26th of that month he was
constituted commander of Guisnes; but within a
short time he was removed, at his own request, to
Boulogne.   The post of commander of Boulogne
required energy, courage, and skill, and there is
ample evidence that the Earl displayed each of those

* See page 63.

qualifications. Many of his despatches describing the
state of affairs at different times are extant, but they
contain little of general interest.   A letter from his
father to him, written in September, justifies the
inference that his representations to the King, urging him to retain Boulogne, were not agreeable to
the Privy Council : —

"TO MY SON OF SURREY.

"WITH this ye shall receive your letter sent to
me by this bearer; by the which I perceive ye find
yourself grieved for that I declared to the King
such things as Cavendish shewed to me: which I
did by his desire; shewing the same of his behalf
without speaking of you.   And if he will say he
desired not me to shew the King thereof, ye may
[say] he sayeth untruly.   For the King hawking
for a pheasant, he desired me as he went homeward
to declare the same to his Highness.   This is true,
and he taken here not of the best sort.   Ye may be
sure I do not use my doings of any sort that may
turn you to any displeasure.   Have yourself in
await, that ye animate not the King too much for
the keeping of Boulogne; for who so doth, at length
shall get small thanks.   I have so handled the matter, that if any adventure be given to win the new
fortress at Boulogne, ye shall have the charge thereof; and therefore, look well what answer ye make
to the letter from us of the Council.   Confirm not
the enterprises contained in them.

"Having written the premises, Mr. Paget desired me to write to you in no wise to animate the King to keep Boulogne. Upon what grounds he spake it I know not; but I fear ye wrote something too much therein to somebody. And thus with God's blessing and mine, Fare ye well. From Windsor, the 27th of September at night.

"Your loving father,

"T. NORFOLK."

In a postscript to an unimportant letter to Lord Cobham, dated at Boulogne on the 20th of October, 1545, Surrey says,

"Whereas I perceive Sir Edward Wooton's son fantaseth a genet gelding of mine, that standeth at Calais, which is blind and winded, I am ashamed to give him; but if it please him to take him till I be able to give him a better, I shall desire him so to do."

A communication addressed to Sir William Paget, on the 20th of the following month, will be inserted, as it shews the zeal with which the Earl advocated the interests of his friends:—

"It may like you, gentle Mr. Secretary, to give me leave, amid your weighty affairs, to trouble you with an earnest suit. Whereas Mr. Treasurer of Guisnes is discharged, and some other, as I hear, appointed to his place, it will please you to inform yourself by the report of such as knoweth, [of] a gentleman, sometime my servant, and now a captain within this

town, called T. Shelley, what his conditions and
qualities are, and disposition to service, and then to
square within yourself whether it be meet to recom-
mend for that office such one, at the most effectual
request of your poor friend, of whose rare virtues
I could write more at large, but that I know virtue
for the self, is to you sufficiently recommended; and
that Mr. Palmer awaiteth upon you, who can sufficiently of the ability of the man instruct you.   Assuring you, Sir, that I dare promise more of that man,
his truth and honesty, than of any man that I know
alive; and I should think myself happy to have
bred such a servant, as I trust his Majesty should
find him.   And for your favour to be granted that
man, I shall most heartily beseech you, and think
the pleasure done as to myself, praying you to pardon my earnest writing: for the worthiness of the
man bears it.   And thus leaving to trouble you, I
pray to God to send you health.   From Boulogne,
the 20th of November.

" Your own most assuredly,

" H. SURREY."

Surrey having received intimation early in January, 1545–6, that the French were about to advance
from Montreuil to re-victual the fortress, he marched
from Boulogne with great part of the garrison to
intercept them near St. Etienne.   Though he was
inferior in numbers, he gallantly attacked the French
troops ; but, in consequence of the cowardice of one

division of his forces, who fled in confusion, notwithstanding all the Earl's efforts to rally them, the
English were defeated, and forced to retreat to Boulogne.

Surrey's despatch to the King, giving an account
of this affair, is as follows:—

"It may like your most excellent Majesty; that
having certain espial that Monsieur Du Biez was
set fort [forth] of Montreuil with six hundred
horse, and three thousand footmen, to relieve the
great necessity of the fortress, mentioned in our
former letters; we took yesterday before day the
trenches at St. Etienne, with six hundred footmen,
and sent out Mr. Ellerkar with all the horsemen of
this town, and Mr. Pollard with two hundred, that
he brought the night before from Guisnes, to discover whither their camp marched, which he had
discovered by their fires at Nouclier over night, six
miles on this side Montreuil. And as they passed
by Hardelot, Mr. Pollard was hurt with a culverin
in the knee, and died thereof the night following;
of whom your Majesty had a notable loss.

"Our horsemen discovered their march beyond
Hardelot, whereupon I, the Earl of Surrey, being
advertised, according to the order agreed upon
amongst us, issued out with Mr. Bridges, Sir Henry
Palmer, Sir Thomas Palmer, Sir Thomas Wyatt,
and two thousand footmen; leaving within your
Majesty's pieces two thousand footmen, and the rest
of the council here, divided in the pieces. And by

that time that we had set our horsemen and footmen in order of battle, without the trench of St.
Etienne, the enemy was also in order of battle on this
side Hardelot, and had put on their carriages by the
sea's side, towards the fortress. Whereupon, having
discovered their horsemen not above five hundred,
and footmen about four thousand, pondering the
weight of the service, which might have imported
no less success than the winning of the fortress; and
the courage and good-will ·that seemed in our men
(the surety of your Majesty's pieces being provided
for) upon a consultation we presented them the fight
with a squadre of pikes and bills, about three score
in file, and two wings of harquebussiers, and one of
bows; and our horsemen on the right wing. Many of
the captains and gentlemen were in the first rank by
their desire; for because they were well armed in
corselets. The battle of the Almains came towards
us likewise with two wings of harquebussiers and
two troops of horsemen.

"Mr. Marshall, Mr. Bellingham, Mr. Porter, Mr.
Shelley, and Mr. Granado, with all the horsemen of
this town, and Guisnes, gave the charge upon their
right flank, and brake their harquebussiers. Their
horsemen fled and ours followed the victory, and
killed and slew till they came to the carriages,
where they brake four score and ten, accompted
by tale this morning. Our squadre then joined
with the Almains, with a cry of as great courage,
and in as good order as we could wish. And by

that time our first rank and the second were come
to the push of the pike, there grew a disorder in our
men, and without cause fled; at which time many
of our gentlemen were slain, which gave as hardy
an onset as hath been seen, and could but have had
good success, if they had been followed. So, stinted
they never for any devise that we could use, till
they came to the trenches: and being well settled
there, which is such a place as may be kept against
all their camp, they forsook that and took the river,
which gave the enemy courage to follow them: albeit the night drawing then on, they followed not
far beyond. Assuring your Majesty that the fury
of their flight was such, that it booted little the
travail that was taken upon every strait to stay
them. And so seeing it not possible to stop them,
we suffered them to retire to the town. In this
meanwhile, our horsemen thinking all won, finding
the disorder, were fain to pass over at a passage a
mile beneath Pont de Brique, without any loss,
having slain a great number of the enemies; whereof we have yet no certain advertisement.

"Thus was there loss and victory on both sides.
And this morning we sent over afore day to number
the dead. There was slain of our side two hundred
and five; whereof captains Mr. Edward Poynings,
Captain Story, Captain Jones, Spencer, Roberts,
Basford, Wourth, Wynchcombe, Mr. Vawse, and a
man at arms called Harvy. Captain Crayford and
Mr. John Palmer, and Captain Shelley, and Cap-

tain Cobham, missed but not found.   All these were
slain in the first rank.   Other there were that escaped.   Among whom Mr. Wyatt was one; assuring your Majesty that there were never gentlemen
served more hardily, if it had chanced, and saving
the disorder of our footmen that fled without cause,
when all things almost seemed won.   The enemy
took more loss than we, but for the gentlemen;
whose loss was much to be lamented.   And this
day we have kept the field from the break of day;
and the enemy retired to Montreuil immediately
after the fight, and left their carriages distressed
behind them.   And not twenty carts entered into
the fortress; and that biscuit.

  " Beseeching your Majesty, though the success
hath not been such as we wished, to accept the good
intent of us all; considering that it seemed to us, in
a matter of such importance, a necessary thing to
present the fight.   And that Mr. Ellerkar may
know we have humbly recommended his good service unto your Highness; which was such, as if all
the rest had answered to the same, the enemy had
been utterly discomforted; and that it may please
your Majesty to give him credit for the declaration
thereof more at large.   Further; whereas Mr.
Henry Dudley was one of those of the first rank
that gave the onset upon the enemy, and is a man
[to be esteemed] for his knowledge, heart, and of
good service, it may like your Highness to be his
good and gracious Lord; that whereas Mr. Poyn-

ings, late captain of your Majesty's guard here is deceased, if your Highness shall think him able to succeed him in that room, at our humble intercession to admit him thereto; if it may so stand with your most gracious pleasure.

"And thus beseeching your Highness to accept our poor service, albeit the success in all things was not such as we wished, yet was the enemies enterprise disappointed, which could not have been otherwise done, and more of their part slain than of ours; and the fortress in as great misery as before, and a sudden flight the let of a full victory. And if any disorder there were, we assure your Majesty there was no default in the rulers, nor lack of courage to be given them, but a humour that sometime reigneth in Englishmen: most humbly thanking your Majesty that it hath pleased the same to consider their payment; which shall much revive their hearts to adventure most willingly their lives, according to their most bounden duty, in your Majesty's service, to make recompense for the disorder that now they have made.

"And thus we pray to God to preserve your most excellent Majesty. From your Highness's town of Boulogne, this 8th of January, 1546.

Your Majesty's most humble
and obedient Servants and Subjects,
H. SURREY.

HUGH POULET. HENRY PALMER.
RICHARD CAVENDISH. JOHN BYRGGYS.
RICHARD WYNDEBANCKE.

" P. S. Whereas we think that this victual can serve for no long time, that they have put into the fortress; wherefore it is to be thought the enemy will attempt the like again shortly: it may please your Majesty to resolve what is further to be done by us; and for the declaration of our poor opinions therein, we have sent Mr. Ellerkar to your Majesty, to whom may it please your Highness to give credit in that behalf; and the present tempest being such, we have thought it meet to send these before, and stay him for a better passage."

His defeat has been supposed to have lessened the good opinion which the King entertained of him, but this is doubtful, as he continued in the command of Boulogne for three months after that event; and, in the beginning of March, he applied to Henry for permission that his wife might join him at Boulogne, which request was refused, on the ground that " time of service, which will bring some trouble and disquietness unmeet for women's imbecilities, approacheth." The first intimation he received that he was to be superseded was in a letter from Secretary Paget, dated about the middle of March, in which there are these passages : —

" My Lord, the latter part of your letter, touching the intended enterprise of the enemy, giveth me occasion to write unto you frankly my poor opinion ; trusting your Lordship will take the same in no worse part than I mean it. As your Lordship wisheth, so his Majesty mindeth to do somewhat for

the endommaging of the enemy : and for that purpose hath appointed to send an army over shortly,
and that my Lord of Hertford shall be his Highness's
Lieutenant General at his being in Boulonnois.
Whereby I fear your authority of Lieutenant shall
be touched : for I believe that the later ordering of
a Lieutenant taketh away the commission of him
that was there before.   Now, my Lord, because you
have been pleased I should write mine advice to
your Lordship in things concerning your honour
and benefit, I could no less do than put you in remembrance how much in mine opinion this shall
touch your honour, if you should pass the thing over
in silence until the very time of my Lord of Hertford's coming over thither; for so should both your
authority be taken away, as I fear is Boulonnois,
and also it should fortune ye to come abroad without any place of estimation in the field; which the
world would much muse at, and, though there be no
such matter, think you were rejected upon occasion
of some either negligence, inexperience, or such other
like fault ; for so many heads so many judgments.
Wherefore, my Lord, in my opinion, you should do
well to make sure by times to his Majesty to appoint
you to some place of service in the army ; as to the
Captainship of the Foreward, or Rearward; or to
such other place of honour as should be meet for
you; for so should you be where knowledge and
experience may be gotten.   Whereby you should
the better be able hereafter to serve, and also to

have peradventure occasion to do some notable service in revenge of your men, at the last encounter with the enemies, which should be to your reputation in the world. Whereas, being hitherto noted as you are a man of a noble courage, and of a desire to shew the same to the face of your enemies, if you should now tarry at home within a wall, having I doubt a shew of your authority touched, it would be thought abroad I fear, that either you were desirous to tarry in a sure place of rest, or else that the credit of your courage and forwardness to serve were diminished; and that you were taken here for a man of [little] activity or service.

"Wherefore, in my opinion, you shall do well, and provide wisely for the conservation of your reputation, to sue to his Majesty for a place of service in the field. Wherein if it shall please you to use me as a mean to his Majesty, I trust so to set forth the matter to his Majesty, as he shall take the same in gracious part, and be content to appoint you to such a place as may best stand with your honour. And this counsel I write unto you as one that would you well; trusting that your Lordship will even so interpret the same, and let me know your mind herein betimes."

Within a few weeks Surrey was summoned to the King's presence to advise on the best mode of fortifying Boulogne; but this command was in fact a civil manner of announcing that he was superseded by the Earl of Hertford.

The next notice which occurs of the Earl is the following letter from him to Secretary Paget, dated on the 14th of July, which is very characteristic. It relates to his conduct whilst commander of Boulogne with respect to the claims of some of the King's servants, as well as of persons to whom Surrey had given certain appointments. His reply to Lord Grey's insinuation that he had himself derived a profit from them is written with all the dignity of conscious integrity : " There are," he says, "in Boulogne too many witnesses that Henry of Surrey was never corrupted by personal considerations, and that his hand never closed upon a bribe : a lesson," he adds, " which he learnt from his father, whom he desired to imitate in this as in all other things."

To the Right Worshipful Sir William Paget, Kt. one of his Majesty's Principal Secretaries :—

"It may like you, with my hearty commendations; that whereas yesternight I perceived by you, that the King's Majesty thinketh his liberality sufficiently extended towards the strangers that have served him, I have with fair words done my best so to satisfy them accordingly; assuring you on my faith, that their necessity seemed to me such, as it cost me an hundred ducats of mine own purse, and somewhat else : so that now there resteth nothing to be done but their passports and ready dispatch from

D

you, wherein it may please you to consider their
great charges here.

"And now you shall give me leave to come to
mine own matters.   Coming from Boulogne in such
sort as you know, I left only two of my servants
behind me; John Rosington and Thomas Copeland.
To the said John, for his notable service, I gave the
advantage of the play in Boulogne; to Thomas, the
prefect of the passage: whom my Lord Grey put
immediately out of service after my departure, notwithstanding the letter I obtained from you to him
in their favour.   Upon a better consideration, John
occupieth his room; and my Lord to his own use
occupieth the other's office of the passage; saying,
'That I, and my predecessors there should use the
same to our gain;' (which I assure you is untrue)
and that it should be parcel of the entertainment of
the Deputy; which in Calais was never used, and
is, me seemeth, too near for a Deputy to grate; unless it were for some displeasure borne me.

"Finally, Mr. Secretary, this is the only suit that
I have made you for any thing touching Boulogne
sith my departure; wherefore it may please you,
that if my Lord Grey will needs be passager, and
that the office was no less worth to the said Thomas
than fifty pounds a year, being placed there by a
King's Lieutenant, (which me thinketh a great disorder that a Captain of Boulogne should displace for
any private gain,) yet at the least it may please you

to request my Lord Grey to recompense him with a sum of money in recompense of that, that he hath lost, and purchased so dearly with so many dangers of life; which my said Lord of his liberality cannot refrain to do.

"And for answer, that my said Lord chargeth me to have returned the same to my private profit, in his so saying he can have none honour. For there be in Boulogne too many witnesses that Henry of Surrey was never for singular profit corrupted; nor never yet bribe closed his hand: which lesson I learned of my father; and wish to succeed him therein as in the rest.

"Further; whereas the said Copeland was placed there for his merits by Mr. Southwell, and me, of the guard; and that my said Lord Grey detaineth from him his wages, it may please you, at my hearty request, to grant him your letters for the obtaining thereof; and of the rest, and to pardon my frankness, for that you know it is my natural, to use it with [such as I do hold my friends]. And thus wishing you [to continue ever more] my friend, till I deserve of [any fault of mine the con]trary, I pray to God send you [what ever good your own] heart desireth. From ———— 14th July, 1546.

"Your assured loving friend,

"H. SURREY."

The great influence which the Earl of Hertford possessed was viewed with jealousy by Norfolk and

his son, though they sought to conciliate him by pro-
posing an alliance between the widowed Duchess of
Richmond, whose marriage was never consummated,
and the Earl's brother, Sir Thomas Seymour. This
alliance did not, however, take place, and Surrey,
either from dislike of Hertford or from some other
cause, was not employed under him. Disappointed
ambition, in a person of an impetuous and haughty
temper, generally vents itself in bitter speeches
against the author of a supposed wrong; and Surrey,
after his return to England, towards the end of
March, 1547, often expressed himself with great
asperity about Hertford.

This conduct having reached the King's ears,
Surrey was arrested and imprisoned at Windsor
in July following, when Henry ordered his father
to be apprised of his imprudence. The Duke in
a letter to the Council desired them to thank his
Majesty for informing him of his son's "foolish de-
meanour;" and after expressing pleasure at finding
he had evinced a proper sense of his behaviour,
Norfolk prayed that he might be "earnestly handled,
in order that he may have regard hereafter so to
use himself, that he may give his Majesty no cause
of discontent." Surrey's confinement must have
been short, as he officiated at court early in August,
on the arrival of the French Ambassadors.

Nothing has been discovered relating to the Earl
between this time and the 12th of December, when
he was arrested and sent to the Tower. The real

causes of this measure have not been developed, but when the irritable state of the King's mind and body, and the situation in which the Howard family then stood with respect to the Seymours are considered, it may be easily imagined that the proud and intemperate Surrey would soon afford his enemies the means of accomplishing his destruction. Sir Robert Southwell having declared that he knew certain things affecting the Earl's fidelity to the King, he was summoned from Kenninghall, and accused before Wriothsley, the Earl of Hertford and others of the Privy Council. He positively denied the charges brought against him, and demanded a public trial, or if this were not to be obtained, he asked to be allowed to prove the falsehood of his accuser by fighting him in his shirt. The Council ordered him into confinement; and within a few days both he and his father were sent to the Tower, each being ignorant of the other's arrest. Depositions were taken upon which to ground an indictment, and it is a disgusting fact that the Duchess of Richmond was one of the witnesses against her father and her brother. The Earl of Surrey was accused of high treason under the statute of the 28th of Henry VIII., whereby among other offences, it was enacted, that if any person by speaking, writing, or printing, or by any other act or deed, did any thing to the peril of the King's person or of his heir, or should by any act, speech, or deed, occasion the King to be disturbed in the

possession of his Crown, he should be considered a
traitor.   The indictment then proceeds to recite that
King Edward the Confessor had borne certain arms
which belonged exclusively to that monarch, his progenitors, and successors, Kings of England; that
Henry and all his progenitors had, from time imme-
morial, used and borne the said arms, they being
annexed to the crown of England; that Prince
Edward, the King's son and heir apparent, had
always borne the same arms from the time of his
birth, with the difference of a silver label of three
points, to the said Prince of right belonging, and to
no other subject whatever; that the Earl of Surrey,
unmindful of his allegiance, had, as a false traitor
and public enemy of the King, conspired to withdraw his subjects from their allegiance, and to de-
prive the King of his royal dignity, on the 7th of
October, 1546, in Kenninghall, in the county of
Norfolk, in the house of Thomas, Duke of Norfolk,
his father, by traitorously and openly causing the
said arms of the King, with three silver labels, to
be painted in conjunction with his own proper arms,
thereby intending to repress, destroy, annihilate,
and scandalize the true and undoubted title of the
said Lord, the now King to the crown of this his
realm of England; and also traitorously to disinherit
and interrupt the said Lord Prince Edward of his
true and undoubted title in and to the said crown
of this realm of England, and then and there maliciously, voluntarily, and traitorously giving occasion

whereby the said Lord the now King might be disturbed and interrupted in his said true title to the said crown of this his realm of England, to the scandal, peril, derogation, and contempt of the said Lord the now King and of his said lawful title to his said crown of England.

In proof of this charge Mrs. Holland, the Duke of Norfolk's mistress, deposed in general terms that he had reproached Surrey for his want of skill in quartering his arms. The Duchess of Richmond declared that he had spoken with asperity of Hertford, to whom he attributed his late imprisonment; that he had shown dislike to the new nobility; had complained that the King expressed displeasure for the defeat at Boulogne in the preceding year; that he had dissuaded her from reading too far in the scriptures; and that he had erected an altar in a church at Boulogne: but in the conclusion of her deposition, she maliciously insinuated that the earl had surmounted his arms instead of with a coronet, with what "seemed to her much like a close crown, and a cipher which she took to be the king's cipher, H. R." Sir Edmund Knyvett and Thomas Pope also gave their testimony, but it contained nothing of the slightest importance.

The crime for which this young nobleman was thus arraigned has never been properly examined; and, satisfied with its manifest absurdity, historians as well as the biographers of Surrey have omitted to point out upon what grounds that inference is justified.

The arms of King Edward the Confessor are presumed to have been a blue field charged with a gold cross flory at the ends, between five gold martets, a kind of swallow without legs; but as heraldry was then unknown, it is extremely doubtful if this or any other bearing was used by that monarch. Arms appear to have been used by the kings of England in the reign of Richard the First, who bore a red shield, charged with three gold lions, which have ever since been deemed to be the arms of England. As early as the time of Edward the First, and probably about a century before, the arms of three saints were always borne on banners in the English army, and on all state occasions, namely, those of St. George, the tutelar saint of this country; of St. Edmund, and of St. Edward the Confessor, but neither of those ensigns was deemed to be connected with the sovereignty of England. Richard the Second, however, being actuated by extraordinary veneration for St. Edward the Confessor, chose him for his patron saint, and impaled his arms with those of England and France; and at the same time, he granted the Confessor's arms to be borne per pale with the paternal coats of two or three of the most eminent noblemen of the day, each of whom was descended from the blood royal. One of the persons so distinguished was Thomas Mowbray, Earl of

Nottingham and Duke of Norfolk, the right to whose arms and quarterings was indisputably inherited by the Earl of Surrey, but the right to the coat of the Confessor depends upon whether it was granted to Mowbray for life only, or to him *and his heirs*, a point which has not been ascertained. Conceiving himself, however, entitled to it,* Surrey in marshalling his arms included it with his other numerous quarterings, and the injustice of construing the act into a treasonable design is still more apparent from other circumstances. Neither Henry the Eighth nor any other monarch after Richard the Second, ever used the arms of the Confessor in conjunction with their own, and the statement that Prince Edward then did so with a label, is not supported by any other evidence. Surrey introduced the label as the proper distinction of his arms from those of his father, so that he appears to have done nothing that he was not authorized by law to do; and even at this moment heralds allow the Con-

---

* The Duke of Norfolk stated in his petition to Queen Mary, to have his own and Surrey's attainder reversed: —

" And forasmuch most gracious Sovereign Lady as the offence wherewith your said subject and supplicant was charged, and whereof he was indicted, was for bearing of arms, which he and his ancestors had heretofore of long time and continuance borne, as well within this realm as without, and as well also in the presence of the said late King, as in the presence of divers of his noble progenitors, Kings of England, and which said arms your said supplicant and subject, and his ancestors might lawfully and justly bear and give, as by good and substantial matter of record it may and doth appear."

fessor's arms to several noble families. It is remarkable that whilst this preposterous accusation
was brought against Surrey, he himself bore the
royal arms by virtue of his descent from Thomas
of Brotherton,* the son of Edward the First, whilst
various other noblemen in the reign of Henry the
Eighth quartered the royal arms of England and
France, and two if not more of them, the Duke of
Buckingham and the Earl of Wiltshire, had borne
them, not in the inferior position of the third or
fourth, but in the *first* quarter, as their paternal
arms with impunity, and as a matter of acknowledged
right.†

Surrey was brought to trial at the Guildhall on
the 13th January, 1547, when he defended himself
with singular courage and ability, by impeaching the
evidence brought against him, and urging his right,
on the authority of the Heralds and of precedent, to
bare the obnoxious arms. When a witness asserted

---

* It is a singular fact, that when Henry the Eighth granted
armorial ensigns to Anne Boleyn, then Marchioness of Pembroke,
he took especial care to shew her *royal* and illustrious descent
through *the Howards*, by introducing the arms of Thomas of
Brotherton, son of Edward the First, and of the Warrens, Earls
of Surrey, out of the *Howard* shield. In the arms of Katharine
Howard Henry impaled with his own the same royal quartering
of Brotherton, whilst in further evidence of her royal descent,
one of the quarterings was formed of the arms of France and
England.

† It was for some centuries the Law of Arms, that whenever
a person was entitled to quarter the royal arms, they were to
take precedence of all others by being placed in the first quarter.

that, in a conversation with the Earl, he repeated some strong expression which Surrey had used, together with his own insolent reply, the prisoner made no other observation than by turning to the Jury and saying, "I leave it to you to judge whether it were probable that this man should speak thus to the Earl of Surrey and he not strike him."

But neither eloquence, nor spirit, nor even innocence itself, was likely to avail a man accused of treason in the reign of Henry the Eighth; and the Jury, among whom it is melancholy to find two near relations of his faithful attendant Clere, found him guilty. He was remanded to the Tower, and beheaded on the 21st of January, just eight days after his conviction, and when he was only thirty years of age.

No particulars are preserved of his deportment in prison or on the scaffold; but from the noble spirit he evinced at his trial, and from his general character, it cannot be doubted that he behaved in the last scene of his existence with fortitude and dignity. On the barbarous injustice to which he was sacrificed comment is unnecessary, but regret at his early fate is increased by the circumstance that Henry himself, whose name is a disgrace to any country, in any age, was in extremities when he ordered his execution, and dying within the same week the life of the Duke of Norfolk was preserved. Surrey was buried in the church of All Hallows-Barking, Tower Street, but his body was, it has been said,

removed to Framlingham by his son, the Earl of
Northampton, where he erected a handsome monument to his father's memory, with this inscription: —

HENRICO . HOWARDO . THOMÆ . SECUNDI . DUCIS

NORFOLCIÆ . FILIO . PRIMOGENITO . THOMÆ . TERTII

PATRI . COMITI . SURRIÆ . ET . GEORGIANI . ORDINIS

EQUITI . AURATO . IMMATURE . ANNO . SALUTIS

MDXLVI . ABREPTO . ET . FRANCISCÆ . UXORI

EJUS . FILIÆ . JOHANNIS . COMITIS . OXONIÆ . 'HENRICUS

HOWARDUS . COMES . NORTHAMPTONIÆ . FILIUS

SECUNDO . GENITUS . HOC . SUPREMUM . PIETATIS

IN . PARENTES . MONUMENTUM . POSUIT

ANNO . DOMINI . MDCXIV.*

Lord Surrey left two sons, Thomas, then about
the age of eleven, who became the fourth Duke of
Norfolk; and Henry, who was created by James
the First, Lord Howard of Marnhill and Earl of
Northampton: and three daughters; Jane who married Charles Neville Earl of Westmoreland, Katharine who married Henry Lord Berkeley, and Margaret who married Henry Lord Scrope of Bolton.
Surrey's widow married secondly, in the reign of
Edward the Sixth, Thomas Steyning, of Woodford,

* The inscription on the monument appears to have been
drawn up by the secretary of the Earl of Northampton, then
lately deceased, "Johanne Griffitho nuper Comit: Northamptoniæ ab epistolis curante," who seems to have been imperfectly
acquainted with the pedigree of his patron; for the Earl of Surrey was son to the *third*, and father to the *fourth* Duke of Norfolk.

in Suffolk, Esq. by whom she had a daughter, Mary, the wife of Charles Seckford, Esq.

A curious inventory of Surrey's apparel is particularly deserving of notice from the manner in which it was distributed among his enemies the Seymours, and others, by the crown, to which it fell by his attainder. These rapacious favourites considered nothing too trifling for their acceptance, and their conduct affords a humiliating idea of a nobleman of the sixteenth century. Both the Protector and his brother partook also very largely of the Duke of Norfolk's jewels and other property.

ALL THESE TO THE DUKE OF SOMERSET. — One Parliament robe of purple velvet, with a garter set upon the shoulder; four black velvet caps, set with pearl and goldsmith's works; a hat of crimson satin and crimson velvet, with a white feather; a scarf of crimson gold, sarcenet; two pairs of knit hose; two dozen arming points; a knit petticoat; two rapiers, all gilt, graven antique; two daggers, all gilt and graven, appendant to two girdles; a gilt dagger, with a sheath of black velvet; a pair of stirrups, all gilt; ditto parcel gilt; another pair of stirrups; two pair of spurs, gilt; a horse harness of black velvet, set with studs, of copper, and gilt; a fod cloth of black velvet, fringed with Venice gold; a horse harness of crimson velvet, fringed with Venice gold.

To MR. COLLEY AND MR. THORP. — A robe, with hood, and crimson velvet.

To MR. BRIAN. — A gown of cloth of gold, furred and faced with sables.

ALL THESE TO SIR HENRY SEYMOUR. — A gown of black velvet, with a curious guard of black satin; a gown of crimson taffeta, faced with busard; a coat and cassock of black velvet, the one wrought with satin, and the other with satin and wreaths; a cape of frizardo, guarded upon with velvet, and embroidered upon with russet satin; with other doublets, hoses, caps, and shirts.

Mr. Fowler. — A gown of black satin embroidered and lined with gold sarcenet; a cassock of black silk embroidered and lined with gold sarcenet.

Mrs. Winfred Fisher. — A robe of black velvet set with buttons of gold enamelled black and white; a pair of hose, black velvet, laid on with threads of Venice gold.

Mr. Philpot. — A robe of black velvet, embroidered with tawney satin; with other doublets and hoses.

Mr. T. Allen. — A doublet of black satin cut.

Mr. Colley and Mr. Thorp. — A shirt wrought with black silk to each.

It is difficult to pronounce a certain opinion upon Surrey's personal character. Dr. Nott and his other biographers have spoken of his merits in a strain of eulogy which, to say the least, is not borne out by the few notices that are preserved of him. That he was accomplished is amply manifested by his works, which also indicate a correct moral taste, since there is not, in the whole of his poems, one word, or an allusion to a single thought, to which the most fastidious person can possibly object. This merit deserves greater praise than it has hitherto received, because he is almost the first English versifier who possessed it; and it is no slight proof of the purity of his mind. Surrey's greatest fault appears to have been a naturally hasty and impetuous temper, which, in a man of exalted rank and great influence was probably increased by his station exacting deference and submission from the greater part of those with whom he came in contact. In his brief career he was imprisoned no less than three times, and ultimately lost his life from his imprudent conduct; and the only excuse which can be made for him is, that he was young, and that he was too proud and too ingenuous to conceal what he thought. His conduct towards the Duchess of Norfolk has been already adverted to, and whatever may have been her errors, the son who could, under any circumstances, treat his mother with unkindness has slight claim to be considered an amiable man. Surrey's military talents and his ardent courage do not admit of being questioned, and his veneration for his father tends, in a slight degree, to redeem his behaviour towards his mother. Examples of his zeal for his friends, and of his deep sense of honour, have been adduced in this memoir, and they certainly entitle his memory to respect, whilst his conduct as a husband and a father has never been impeached.

Of his writings, and the rank to which he is entitled among the poets of England, the remarks of Puttenham, Warton, Henry, and Dr. Nott, contain all which can be said on the subject.

Puttenham says: "In the latter end of Henry the Eighth's reign sprung up a new company of courtly makers, of whom Sir Thomas Wyatt the elder, and Henry Earl of Surrey, were the two chieftains, who having travelled into Italy, and there tasted the sweet and stately measures and style of the Italian poesie, as novices newly crept out of the schools of Dante, Ariosto, and Petrarch, they

greatly polished our rude and homely manner of
vulgar poesie, from that it had been before, and for
that cause may justly be said the first reformers
of our English metre and style.

" Henry Earl of Surrey and Sir Thomas Wyatt,
between whom I find very little difference, I re-
pute them (as before) for the two chief lanterns of
light to all others that have since employed their
pens upon English poesie; their conceits were lofty,
their styles stately, their conveyance cleanly, their
terms proper, their metre sweet and well propor-
tioned, in all imitating very naturally and studiously
their master Francis Petrarcha."

Warton observes: " In the sonnets of Surrey, we
are surprised to find nothing of that metaphysical
cast which marks the Italian poets, his supposed
masters, especially Petrarch. Surrey's sentiments
are for the most part natural and unaffected; arising from his own feelings, and dictated by the present circumstances. His poetry is alike unembar-
rassed by learned allusions, or elaborate conceits.
If our author copies Petrarch, it is Petrarch's better
manner: when he descends from his Platonic ab-
stractions, his refinements of passion, his exaggerated
compliments, and his play upon opposite sentiments,
into a track of tenderness, simplicity, and nature.
Petrarch would have been a better poet had he been
a worse scholar. Our author's mind was not too
much overlaid by learning.

" Surrey's talents, which are commonly supposed

to have been confined to sentiment and amorous lam-
entation, were adapted to descriptive poetry and the
representations of rural imagery. But he was not
merely the poet of idleness and gallantry. He was
fitted, both from nature and study, for the more solid
and laborious parts of literature. He translated the
second and fourth books of Virgil into blank verse:
and it seems probable, that his active situations of
life prevented him from completing a design of trans-
lating the whole Eneid. This is the first composi-
tion in blank verse extant in the English language.
Nor has it merely the relative and accidental merit
of being a curiosity. It is executed with great
fidelity, yet not with a prosaic servility. The diction is often poetical, and the versification varied
with proper pauses. Surrey, for his justness of
thought, correctness of style, and purity of expression,
may justly be pronounced the first English classical
poet. He unquestionably is the first polite writer
of love-verses in our language. It must, however,
be allowed, that there is a striking native beauty in
some of our love-verses written much earlier than
Surrey's. But in the most savage ages and coun-
tries, rude nature has taught elegance to the lover."

Dr. Henry's criticism is no less favourable:
" Poetry revived in England under Henry the
Eighth, and was cultivated by his courtiers as a
vehicle of gallantry; but by none more than the
brave but unfortunate Surrey, who had taste to
relish the Italian poets, and judgment to reject their

E

affected, though splendid conceits. His sonnets
were once celebrated, but are now neglected; unjust-
ly neglected, for their merit is considerable, and
their influence imparted a new character to English
poetry. Surrey was inspired by a genuine passion,
and his sonnets breathe the unaffected dictates of
nature and love. Tenderness predominates in the
sentiment, ease and elegance distinguish the language. From these sonnets, the earliest specimens
of a polished diction and refined sensibility, succeed-
ing poets discovered the capacity and secret powers
of the English tongue. They are not numerous,
though sufficient to effect a reformation in poetry,
nor discriminated always from the sonnets of others;
but of those whose authenticity is certain, the complaint uttered in confinement at Windsor, touches
irresistibly the heart with woe. Blank verse, now
peculiar to English poetry, had been recently attempted in Italian and Spanish, and was first trans-
planted by Surrey into some translations from
Virgil, which discover rather the concinnity of
rhyme than the swelling progression of blank verse."

It is difficult to give extracts from Dr. Nott's
remarks on Surrey's writings, but the following
passages seem to convey all that is material: —

"Surrey perceived that some change in our versification was unavoidable, and he attempted a change,
which was conceived, as the event has proved, in a
perfect knowledge of the nature and genius of the
English language. The change he proposed and

effected was this. He substituted for the old rhyth-
mical 'mode of versification one, as nearly metrical
as the nature of any language, which regulates the
value of syllables by accent, and not by quantity,
will allow. He limited the heroic verse to ten syllables, and these he divided into five equal Iambic
feet; for he perceived that the frequent return of
the short syllable was necessary to correct that lan-
guor and ponderosity which the constant recurrence
of monosyllables would otherwise occasion. He was
aware, however, that the Iambic measure, though
sweet in itself, was liable to become monotonous and
pall upon the ear. · He therefore introduced the
further refinement of breaking the lines with pauses.
The natural place for the pause was at the end of
the fourth syllable where the old cæsura generally
fell; but he varied the situation of his pauses as he
found the harmony of the verse required, or as he
thought the beauty and effect of the passage would.
be heightened by it.

    " Such was the system of versification introduced
by Surrey. Of the correctness of his taste and the
justness of his reasoning upon the subject, no further
proof need be required than the event. For the
laws of English versification, such as they were
established by Surrey, have been adopted by our
standard writers, with hardly any variation, ever
since. At particular times, indeed, a particular taste
has for a short season prevailed. Thus in the reign
of James, and of Charles the First, quaintness, and

a love of antithesis gave a new turn to our versification, and made it abrupt and irregular. But in
the two best epochs of our poetry, during the reign
of Elizabeth and after the Restoration, those prin-
ciples of versification alone were observed which
Surrey had introduced. An attentive reader will
be surprised to find how little was added afterwards
by even Dryden or Pope to the system and perfectness of Surrey's numbers.

" Surrey first rejected the use of those ' aureate
and mellifluate ' terms, which he found disfiguring
our language with a sort of prescriptive tyranny,
and restricted himself to the use of those words alone
which were approved by common use, and were
natural to the language.

" He next introduced a studied mode of involution
in his periods, which gives dignity to what is so
expressed, and a certain remoteness from common
life, essential to the higher branches of poetic com-
position. And lastly, he discountenanced altogether
the French mode of laying an unnatural stress upon
final syllables; he followed the obvious and common
pronunciation of our language; carefully avoiding
all double terminations, and using only those words
for rhyme which were noble and harmonious, and
such as the ear might dwell upon with pleasure.

" Such were the improvements made by Surrey
in our versification and poetic diction. These alone,
had nothing more been effected by him, would have
entitled him to the praise of having been the restorer

of modern English poetry. But we owe to him
further obligations. He first introduced the use
of Blank Heroic Verse. In this respect the praise
is exclusively his own. In reforming our versification and poetic diction, he had in some degree
Chaucer for his guide; and in some degree he was
conducted by the bent and genius of our language.
When he attempted blank verse he had no guide
whatever, as far as we have yet been able to discover, but his own judgment and taste. All writers
are agreed that Surrey's translation of the Second
and Fourth Book of Virgil's Æneid is the first
specimen of Heroic Blank Verse in our language.

"The leading features of Surrey's style were
chiefly dignity and compression. Of his compression,
contrasted with the diffusive mode of writing used
by all the authors who preceded him, a more striking instance cannot well be found than that which
occurs in the opening to his sonnet on Sir Thomas
Wyatt's death.

" The reader's observation will enable him easily
to collect from Surrey's poems other instances of
elegant and nervous compression. I do not recollect
a single passage where a thought is needlessly
expanded for the sake of filling up a line. Surrey's
style bears a stronger resemblance to Dryden's than
to that of any other of our poets. The same manli-
ness, and ease, and vigour characterizes both. In
neither do we find any affectation of prettiness;
they seem both to have been more intent on their

thoughts than their words; they gave their words, indeed, a full and a due consideration, but, as always ought to be the case, in subserviency to their thoughts.

" It now remains to shew, that I have not laboured to give a higher importance to Surrey's writings, than they in reality possess. But how shall we appreciate his writings too highly, who by a single effort of genius corrected a nation's taste, and shewed them first the way to that perfection in poetry, to which they have since attained? That the great change which in the sixteenth century took place in our national poetry, was owing chiefly to the influence of Surrey's writings, seems to me incontestable from the general popularity which they obtained immediately upon their appearance: and the studied imitation of them to be traced in all our poets in succession, from Sackville down to Spenser.

" Of the popularity of Surrey's poems, we have a convincing proof in the rapidity with which editions were multiplied. They were first printed in June, 1557. In the course of that and the following month they went through no less than four distinct impressions. They were afterwards reprinted in 1565, in 1567, and in 1569, twice afterwards in 1574, again in 1585, and again 1587. Besides this, selections from Surrey's poems were printed almost daily, with other popular pieces in single sheets, and in small collections called garlands; by means of which they were made familiar to readers of the lower

orders : whilst some of them, as we learn from the
books of the Stationers' Company, were moralized ;
a circumstance which of itself is sufficient to prove
their popularity, and extensive circulation.* In
addition to these facts we are to consider yet further,
that Surrey's verses continued to be multiplied in
manuscript by many who had not the means of
purchasing printed copies ; and that they uniformly
made part of all the printed miscellanies of those
days, up to the beginning of the seventeenth century.
It would be difficult to find an instance of any poet
in any country whose works were in so short a time
more widely circulated.   And if so, we might ask,
whether it would be . possible 'that writings thus
largely diffused, and thus universally admired, should
not produce a general and a lasting effect on public
taste."   .

   The present edition has been printed from the '
collection of Surrey's pieces by Tottel in 1557,
which was the first that appeared, and some explanation is necessary why Dr. Nott's text was not
adopted.   It appears that that writer has made
many alterations without any apparent authority,
and not a few of the variations seem to be as inju-

---

* " Surrey's pleasing little ode, ' When raging love with extreme pain,' which seems to have been a very popular piece,
was printed in 1568 by J. Alde, moralized into ' When raging
lust,' &c. ' Give place, ye ladies,' etc. was often reprinted as a
ballad."

dicious as they were arbitrary. In those cases, however, where a better reading is given by Nott from the Harington MS., or where an alteration was called for on account of the obscurity of a passage arising from a typographical error, the emendation of that indefatigable biographer of the noble Surrey has been followed. The authority for the title of each piece is that of the first, and indeed every other edition, excepting the one by Dr. Nott.*

---

* The following examples of the manner in which the titles of some of the poems have been altered by Dr. Nott are sufficient to show the erroneous conclusions into which he is likely to lead his readers:—

"The Complaint of the Lover disdained," is called by Dr. Nott, "To account for Geraldine's growing indifference and the increase of his own passion, Surrey supposes her to have drunk of the fountain of aversion, and himself of the fountain of love."

"The frailty and hurtfulness of beauty," is entitled by Dr. Nott, "Repulsed by the Fair Geraldine with scorn and cruelty, Surrey inveighs against beauty itself, as a dangerous gift, and one which reason ought not to covet."

The Sonnet, "To the Lady that scorned her Lover," is called by Nott, "Confident of his power to recover his liberty, Surrey again exults at having broke his chains, and again warns the Fair Geraldine to beware of his resentment."

The Poem, "On a Lady that refused to dance with him," Dr. Nott has entitled, "Surrey renounces all affection for the fair Geraldine."

SONGS AND SONNETS.

DESCRIPTION OF THE RESTLESS STATE

OF A LOVER, WITH SUIT TO HIS LADY, TO RUE ON HIS DYING HEART.

THE sun hath twice brought forth his tender green,
Twice clad the earth in lively lustiness;
Once have the winds the trees despoiled clean,
And once again begins their cruelness;
Since I have hid under my breast the harm
That never shall recover healthfulness.
The winter's hurt recovers with the warm;
The parched green restored is with shade;
What warmth, alas! may serve for to disarm
The frozen heart, that mine in flame hath made?
What cold again is able to restore
My fresh green years, that wither thus and fade?
Alas! I see nothing hath hurt so sore
But Time, in time, reduceth a return:
In time my harm increaseth more and more,
And seems to have my cure always in scorn.
Strange kinds of death in life that I do try!
At hand, to melt; far off in flame to burn.
And like as time list to my cure apply,

1

So doth each place my comfort clean refuse.
All thing alivè, that seeth the heavens with eye,
With cloak of night, may cover, and excuse
It self from travail of the day's unrest,
Save I, alas! against all others use,
That then stir up the torments of my breast;
And curse each star as causer of my fate.
And when the sun hath eke the dark opprest,
And brought the day, it doth nothing abate
The travails of mine endless smart and pain.
For then, as one that hath the light in hate,
I wish for night, more covertly to plain;
And me withdraw from every haunted place,
Lest by my chere my chance appear too plain.
And in my mind I measure pace by pace,
To seek the place where I myself had lost,
That day that I was tangled in the lace,
In seeming slack, that knitteth ever most.
But never yet the travail of my thought,
Of better state, could catch a cause to boast.
For if I found, some time that I have sought,
Those stars by whom I trusted of the port,
My sails do fall, and I advance right nought;
As anchor'd fast my spirits do all resort
To stand agazed, and sink in more and more [1]
The deadly harm which she doth take in sport.
Lo! if I seek, how I do find my sore!
And if I flee, I carry with me still

---

[1] To stand *at gaze* and *suck* in more and more. MSS. cited
by Dr. Nott.

The venom'd shaft, which doth his force restore
By haste of flight; and I may plain my fill
Unto myself, unless this careful song
Print in your heart some parcel of my tene.[1]
For I, alas! in silence all too long,
Of mine old hurt yet feel the wound but green.
Rue on my Life; or else your cruel wrong
Shall well appear, and by my death be seen.

———◆———

DESCRIPTION OF SPRING,

WHEREIN EVERY THING RENEWS, SAVE ONLY THE LOVER.

THE soote[2] season, that bud and bloom forth brings,
With green hath clad the hill, and eke the vale.
The nightingale with feathers new she sings;
The turtle to her make[3] hath told her tale.
Summer is come, for every spray now springs,
The hart hath hung his old head on the pale;
The buck in brake his winter coat he slings;
The fishes flete with new repaired scale;
The adder all her slough away she slings;
The swift swallow pursueth the flies smale;[4]
The busy bee her honey now she mings;[5]
Winter is worn that was the flowers' bale.[6]
  And thus I see among these pleasant things
  Each care decays, and yet my sorrow springs!

[1] i. e. Sorrow.   [2] Sweet.   [3] Mate.
[4] Small.   [5] Mingles.   [6] Destruction.

DESCRIPTION OF THE RESTLESS STATE OF
A LOVER.

WHEN youth had led me half the race
That Cupid's scourge had made me run;
I looked back to mete the place
From whence my weary course begun.

And then I saw how my desire
By guiding ill had led the way:
Mine eyen, too greedy of their hire,
Had made me lose a better prey.

For when in sighs I spent the day,
And could not cloak my grief with game;
The boiling smoke did still bewray
The present heat of secret flame.

And when salt tears do bain my breast,
Where Love his pleasant trains hath sown;
Her beauty hath the fruits opprest,
Ere that the buds were sprung and blown.

And when mine eyen did still pursue
The flying chase of their request;
Their greedy looks did oft renew
The hidden wound within my breast.

When every look these cheeks might stain,
From deadly pale to glowing red;
By outward signs appeared plain,
To her for help my heart was fled.

But all too late Love learneth me
To paint all kind of colours new;
To blind their eyes that else should see
My speckled cheeks with Cupid's hue.

And now the covert breast I claim,
That worshipp'd Cupid secretly;
And nourished his sacred flame,
From whence no blazing sparks do fly.

———◆———

DESCRIPTION OF THE FICKLE AFFECTIONS, PANGS, AND SLIGHTS OF LOVE.

Such wayward ways hath Love, that most part
    in discord
Our wills do stand, whereby our hearts but seldom
    do accord.
Deceit is his delight, and to beguile and mock
The simple hearts, which he doth strike with fro-
    ward, diverse stroke.
He causeth the one to rage with golden burning dart;
And doth allay with leaden cold again the other's
    heart.

Hot gleams of burning fire, and easy sparks of flame,
In balance of unequal weight he pondereth by aim.
From easy ford, where I might wade and pass full
　　　well,
He me withdraws, and doth me drive into a deep
　　　dark hell;
And me withholds where I am call'd and offer'd
　　　place,
And wills me that my mortal foe I do beseech of
　　　grace;
He lets me to pursue a conquest well near won,
To follow where my pains were lost, ere that my
　　　suit begun.
So by these means I know how soon a heart may
　　　turn
From war to peace, from truce to strife, and so
　　　again return.
I know how to content myself in others lust;
Of little stuff unto myself to weave a web of trust;
And how to hide my harms with soft dissembling
　　　chere,
When in my face the painted thoughts would out-
　　　wardly appear.
I know how that the blood forsakes the face for
　　　dread;
And how by shame it stains again the cheeks with
　　　flaming red.
I know under the green, the serpent how he lurks;
The hammer of the restless forge I wot eke how
　　　it works.

I know, and can by rote the tale that I would tell;
But oft the words come forth awry of him that
    loveth well.
I know in heat and cold the lover how he shakes;
In singing how he doth complain; in sleeping how
    he wakes.
To languish without ach, sickless for to consume,
A thousand things for to devise, resolving all in
    fume.
And though he list to see his lady's grace full sore;
Such pleasures as delights his eye, do not his health
    restore.
I know to seek the track of my desired foe,
And fear to find that I do seek. But chiefly this
    I know,
That lovers must transform into the thing beloved,
And live, (alas! who could believe?) with sprite
    from life removed.
I know in hearty sighs, and laughters of the spleen,
At once to change my state, my will, and eke my
    colour clean.
I know how to deceive myself with others help;
And how the lion chastised is, by beating of the
    whelp.
In standing near the fire, I know how that I freeze;
Far off I burn; in both I waste, and so my life I
    lese.
I know how love doth rage upon a yielding mind;
How small a net may take, and meash a heart of
    gentle kind:

Or else with seldom sweet to season heaps of gall;
Revived with a glimpse of grace, old sorrows to let
    fall.
The hidden trains I know, and secret snare of love;
How soon a look will print a thought, that never
    may remove.
The slipper state I know, the sudden turns from
    wealth;
The doubtful hope, the certain woe, and sure de-
    spair of health.

COMPLAINT OF A LOVER THAT DEFIED LOVE,

AND WAS BY LOVE AFTER THE MORE TORMENTED.

WHEN Summer took in hand the winter to assail,
With force of might, and virtue great, his stormy
    blasts to quail:
And when he clothed fair the earth about with
    green,
And every tree new garmented, that pleasure was
    to seen:
Mine heart gan new revive, and changed blood did
    stir,
Me to withdraw my winter woes, that kept within
    the dore.[1]

[1] Door.

'Abroad,' quoth my desire, 'assay to set thy foot;
Where thou shalt find the savour sweet; for sprung
    is every root.
And to thy health, if thou were sick in any case,
Nothing more good than in the spring the air to feel
    a space.
There shalt thou hear and see all kinds of birds
    y-wrought,
Well tune their voice with warble small, as nature
    hath them taught.'
Thus pricked me my lust the sluggish house to
    leave,
And for my health I thought it best such counsel to
    receive.
So on a morrow forth, unwist of any wight,
I went to prove how well it would my heavy burden
    light.
And when I felt the air so pleasant round about,
Lord! to myself how glad I was that I had gotten
    out.
There might I see how Ver[1] had every blossom
    hent,[2]
And eke the new betrothed birds, y-coupled how
    they went;
And in their songs, methought, they thanked Nature ·
    much,
That by her license all that year to love, their hap
    was such,

[1] Spring.
[2] Taken hold of, i. e. brought out every blossom.

Right as they could devise to choose them feres [1]
    throughout:
With much rejoicing to their Lord, thus flew they
    all about.   [ceive,
Which when I gan resolve, and in my head con-
What pleasant life, what heaps of joy, these little
    birds receive;
And saw in what estate I, weary man, was wrought,
By want of that, they had at will, and I reject at
    nought;
Lord! how I gan in wrath unwisely me demean!
I cursed Love, and him defied; I thought to turn
    the stream.
But when I well beheld, he had me under awe,
I asked mercy for my fault, that so transgrest his
    law:
'Thou blinded God,' quoth I, 'forgive me this
    offence,
Unwittingly I went about, to malice thy pretence.'
Wherewith he gave a beck, and thus methought he
    swore:
'Thy sorrow ought suffice to purge thy fault, if it
    were more.'
The virtue of which sound mine heart did so revive,
That I, methought, was made as whole as any man
    alive.
But here I may perceive mine error, all and some,
For that I thought that so it was; yet was it still
    undone;

---

[1] Companions, mates.

And all that was no more but mine expressed mind,
That fain would have some good relief, of Cupid
    well assign'd.
I turned home forthwith, and might perceive it well,
That he aggrieved was right sore with me for my
    rebel.
My harms have ever since increased more and
    more,   [more.
And I remain, without his help undone, for ever
A mirror let me be unto ye lovers all;
Strive not with love; for if ye do, it will ye thus
    befall.

—◆—

COMPLAINT OF A LOVER REBUKED.

Love, that liveth and reigneth in my thought,
That built his seat within my captive breast;
Clad in the arms wherein with me he fought,
Oft in my face he doth his banner rest.
She, that me taught to love, and suffer pain;
My doubtful hope, and eke my hot desire
With shamefaced cloak to shadow and restrain,
Her smiling grace converteth straight to ire.
And coward Love then to the heart apace
Taketh his flight; whereas he lurks, and plains
His purpose lost, and dare not shew his face.
For my Lord's guilt thus faultless bide I pains.
    Yet from my Lord shall not my foot remove:
    Sweet is his death, that takes his end by love.

COMPLAINT OF THE LOVER DISDAINED.

IN Cyprus springs, whereas Dame Venus dwelt,
A well so hot, that whoso tastes the same,
Were he of stone, as thawed ice should melt,
And kindled find his breast with fixed flame;
Whose moist poison dissolved hath my hate.
This creeping fire my cold limbs so opprest,
That in the heart that harbour'd freedom, late:
Endless despair long thraldom hath imprest.
Another [1] so cold in frozen ice is found,
Whose chilling venom of repugnant kind,
The fervent heat doth quench of Cupid's wound,
And with the spot of change infects the mind;
   Whereof my dear hath tasted to my pain:
   My service thus is grown into disdain.[2]

DESCRIPTION AND PRAISE OF HIS LOVE GERALDINE.

FROM Tuscane came my Lady's worthy race;
Fair Florence was sometime her [3] ancient seat.
The western isle whose pleasant shore doth face
Wild Camber's cliffs, did give her lively heat.
Foster'd she was with milk of Irish breast:
Her sire an Earl; her dame of Prince's blood.

---

[1] *Sc.* Well.
[2] Whereby my service grows into disdain. — *Nott's Ed.*
[3] *i. e.* Their.

From tender years, in Britain doth she rest,
With Kinges child; where she tasteth costly food.
Hunsdon did first present her to mine eyen:
Bright is her hue, and Geraldine she hight.
Hampton me taught to wish her first for mine;
And Windsor, alas! doth chase me from her sight.
   Her beauty of kind; her virtues from above;
   Happy is he that can obtain her love!

THE FRAILTY AND HURTFULNESS OF BEAUTY.[1]

BRITTLE beauty, that Nature made so frail,
Whereof the gift is small, and short is the season;
Flowering to-day, to-morrow apt to fail;
Tickle treasure, abhorred of reason:
Dangerous to deal with, vain, of none avail;
Costly in keeping, past not worth two peason;[2]
Slipper in sliding, as is an eel's tail;
Hard to obtain, once gotten, not geason:[3]
Jewel of jeopardy, that peril doth assail;
False and untrue, enticed oft to treason;
Enemy to youth, that most may I bewail;
Ah! bitter sweet, infecting as the poison,
   Thou farest as fruit that with the frost is taken;
   To-day ready ripe, to-morrow all to shaken.

1 In the Harrington MS. this poem is attributed to Lord Vaux.
2 Two pease.   3 Rare, or uncommon.

A COMPLAINT BY NIGHT OF THE LOVER NOT BELOVED.

ALAS! so all things now do hold their peace!
Heaven and earth disturbed in no thing;
The beasts, the air, the birds their song do cease,
The nightès car the stars about doth bring.
Calm is the sea; the waves work less and less:
So am not I, whom love, alas! doth wring,
Bringing before my face the great increase
Of my desires, whereat I weep and sing,
In joy and woe, as in a doubtful case.
For my sweet thoughts sometime do pleasure bring;
But by and by, the cause of my disease
Gives me a pang, that inwardly doth sting,
   When that I think what grief it is again,
   To live and lack the thing should rid my pain.

HOW EACH THING, SAVE THE LOVER IN SPRING, REVIVETH TO PLEASURE.

WHEN Windsor walls sustain'd my wearied arm;
My hand my chin, to ease my restless head;
The pleasant plot revested green with warm;
The blossom'd boughs, with lusty Ver [1] y-spread;
The flower'd meads, the wedded birds so late

1 Spring.

Mine eyes discover; and to my mind resort
The jolly woes, the hateless, short debate,
The rakehell[1] life, that 'longs to love's disport.
Wherewith, alas! the heavy charge of care
Heap'd in my breast breaks forth, against my will
In smoky sighs, that overcast the air.
My vapour'd eyes such dreary tears distil,
  The tender spring which quicken where they fall;
  And I half bend to throw me down withal.

A VOW TO LOVE FAITHFULLY, HOWSOEVER HE BE REWARDED.

SET me whereas the sun doth parch the green,
Or where his beams do not dissolve the ice;
In temperate heat, where he is felt and seen;
In presence prest[2] of people, mad, or wise;
Set me in high, or yet in low degree;
In longest night, or in the shortest day;
In clearest sky, or where clouds thickest be;
In lusty youth, or when my hairs are gray:
Set me in heaven, in earth, or else in hell,
In hill, or dale, or in the foaming flood;
Thrall, or at large, alive whereso I dwell,.
Sick, or in health, in evil fame or good,
  Her's will I be; and only with this thought
  Content myself, although my chance be nought.

1 Careless.
2 Query, press, i. e. in the presence of a crowd of people.

COMPLAINT THAT HIS LADY,

AFTER SHE KNEW HIS LOVE, KEPT HER FACE ALWAYS HIDDEN FROM HIM.

I NEVER saw my Lady lay apart
Her cornet [1] black, in cold nor yet in heat,
Sith first she knew my grief was grown so great;
Which other fancies driveth from my heart,
That to myself I do the thought reserve,
The which unwares did wound my woful breast;
But on her face mine eyes might never rest.
Yet since she knew I did her love and serve,
Her golden tresses clad alway with black,
Her smiling looks that hid thus evermore,
And that restrains which I desire so sore.
So doth this cornet govern me alack!
   In summer, sun, in winter's breath, a frost;
   Whereby the light of her fair looks I lost.

REQUEST TO HIS LOVE TO JOIN BOUNTY WITH BEAUTY.

THE golden gift that Nature did thee give,
To fasten friends and feed them at thy will,
With form and favour, taught me to believe,
How thou art made to shew her greatest skill.

[1] A head dress, with a hood or veil attached to it.

Whose hidden virtues are not so unknown,
But lively dooms [1] might gather at the first
Where beauty so her perfect seed hath sown,
Of other graces follow needs there must.
Now certes, Garret, [2] since all this is true,
That from above thy gifts are thus elect,
Do not deface them then with fancies new;
Nor change of minds, let not the mind infect:
But mercy him thy friend that doth thee serve;
Who seeks alway thine honour to preserve.

———◆———

PRISONED IN WINDSOR, HE RECOUNTETH HIS PLEASURE THERE PASSED.

So cruel prison how could betide, alas,
As proud Windsor, where I in lust and joy,
With a Kinges son, my childish years did pass,
In greater feast than Priam's sons of Troy.

[1] Judgments.
[2] Dr. Nott observes, "The first quarto and all the other editions, except the second and third quartos, read 'Now certes, Lady.' Why the genuine reading given in the text should have ever been suppressed it is difficult to say. The Fitz-Gerald family almost always wrote their name Garret. The Fair Geraldine, when attending on the Princess Mary, was always called Garret: and she herself in her Will designates her sister, the Lady Margaret Fitz-Gerald, 'The Lady Margaret Garret.'"

2

Where each sweet place returns a taste full sour.
The large green courts, where we were wont to
   hove,[1]
With eyes cast up into the Maiden's tower,
And easy sighs, such as folk draw in love.
The stately seats, the ladies bright of hue.
The dances short, long tales of great delight;
With words and looks, that tigers could but rue;
Where each of us did plead the other's right.
The palme-play,[2] where, despoiled for the game,
With dazed eyes oft we by gleams of love
Have miss'd the ball, and got sight of our dame,
To bait her eyes, which kept the leads above.
The gravel'd ground, with sleeves tied on the helm,
On foaming horse, with swords and friendly hearts;
With chere, as though one should another whelm,
Where we have fought, and chased oft with darts.
With silver drops the mead yet spread for ruth,
In active games of nimbleness and strength,
Where we did strain, trained with swarms of youth,
Our tender limbs, that yet shot up in length.
The secret groves, which oft we made resound
Of pleasant plaint, and of our ladies' praise;
Recording oft what grace each one had found,
What hope of speed, what dread of long delays.
The wild forest, the clothed holts with green;
With reins availed, and swift y-breathed horse,
With cry of hounds, and merry blasts between,

---

[1] Hover.   [2] Tennis-court.

Where we did chase the fearful hart of force.
The void vales [1] eke, that harbour'd us each night:
Wherewith, alas! reviveth in my breast
The sweet accord, such sleeps as yet delight;
The pleasant dreams, the quiet bed of rest;
The secret thoughts, imparted with such trust;
The wanton talk, the divers change of play;
The friendship sworn, each promise kept so just,
Wherewith we past the winter night away.
And with this thought the blood forsakes the face;
The tears berain [2] my cheeks of deadly hue:
The which, as soon as sobbing sighs, alas!
Up-supped have, thus I my plaint renew:
'O place of bliss! renewer of my woes!
Give me account, where is my noble fere? [3]
Whom in thy walls thou dost each night enclose;
To other [4] lief; but unto me most dear.'
Echo, alas! that doth my sorrow rue,
Returns thereto a hollow sound of plaint.
Thus I alone, where all my freedom grew,
In prison pine, with bondage and restraint:
And with remembrance of the greater grief,
To banish the less, I find my chief relief.

[1] According to Dr. Nott, this line in the Harrington MS. reads thus,

> The *void walls* eke, that harbour'd us each night.

[2] Bedew, as with rain.   [3] Companion.   [4] Endeared.

THE LOVER COMFORTETH HIMSELF WITH THE WORTHINESS OF HIS LOVE.

WHEN raging love with extreme pain
Most cruelly distrains my heart;
When that my tears, as floods of rain,
Bear witness of my woful smart;
When sighs have wasted so my breath
That I lie at the point of death:

I call to mind the navy great
That the Greeks brought to Troy town:
And how the boisterous winds did beat
Their ships, and rent their sails adown;
Till Agamemnon's daughter's blood
Appeas'd the Gods that them withstood.

And how that in those ten years war
Full many a bloody deed was done;
And many a lord that came full far,
There caught his bane, alas! too soon;
And many a good knight overrun,
Before the Greeks had Helen won.

Then think I thus: 'Sith such repair,
So long time war of valiant men,
Was all to win a lady fair,
Shall I not learn to suffer then?

And think my life well spent to be,
Serving a worthier wight than she?'

Therefore I never will repent,
But pains contented still endure;
For like as when, rough winter spent,
The pleasant spring straight draweth in ure;
So after raging storms of care,
Joyful at length may be my fare.

----&----

COMPLAINT OF THE ABSENCE OF HER LOVER BEING UPON THE SEA.

O HAPPY dames that may embrace
The fruit of your delight;
Help to bewail the woful case,
And eke the heavy plight,
Of me, that wonted to rejoice
The fortune of my pleasant choice:
Good ladies! help to fill my mourning voice.

In ship freight with remembrance
Of thoughts and pleasures past,
He sails that hath in governance
My life while it will last;
With scalding sighs, for lack of gale,
Furthering his hope, that is his sail,
Toward me, the sweet port of his avail.

Alas! how oft in dreams I see
Those eyes that were my food;
Which sometime so delighted me,
That yet they do me good:
Wherewith I wake with his return,
Whose absent flame did make me burn:
But when I find the lack, Lord! how I mourn.

When other lovers in arms across,
Rejoice their chief delight;
Drowned in tears, to mourn my loss,
I stand the bitter night
In my window, where I may see
Before the winds how the clouds flee:
Lo! what mariner love hath made of me.

And in green waves when the salt flood
Doth rise by rage of wind;
A thousand fancies in that mood
Assail my restless mind.
Alas! now drencheth [1] my sweet foe,
That with the spoil of my heart did go,
And left me; but, alas! why did he so?

And when the seas wax calm again,
To chase from me annoy,
My doubtful hope doth cause me plain;
So dread cuts off my joy.
Thus is my wealth mingled with woe:
And of each thought a doubt doth grow;
Now he comes! will he come? alas! no, no!

[1] Is drowned.

COMPLAINT OF A DYING LOVER

REFUSED UPON HIS LADY'S UNJUST MISTAKING OF HIS
WRITING.

In winter's just return, when Boreas gan his reign,
And every tree unclothed fast, as nature taught
    them plain:
In misty morning dark, as sheep are then in hold,
I hied me fast, it sat me on, my sheep for to unfold.
And as it is a thing that lovers have by fits,
Under a palm I heard one cry as he had lost his wits.
Whose voice did ring so shrill in uttering of his plaint,
That I amazed was to hear how love could him
    attaint.
'Ah! wretched man,' quoth he; 'come, death, and
    rid this woe;
A just reward, a happy end, if it may chance thee so.
Thy pleasures past have wrought thy woe without
    redress;
If thou hadst never felt no joy, thy smart had been
    the less.'
And rechless of his life, he gan both sigh and groan:
A rueful thing me thought it was, to hear him make
    such moan.
'Thou cursed pen,' said he, 'woe-worth the bird thee
    bare;
The man, the knife, and all that made thee, woe be
    to their share:

Woe-worth the time and place where I so could
    indite;
And woe be it yet once again, the pen that so can
    write.
Unhappy hand! it had been happy time for me,
If when to write thou learned first, unjointed hadst
    thou be.'
Thus cursed he himself, and every other wight,
Save her alone whom love him bound to serve both
    day and night.
Which when I heard, and saw how he himself for-
    did;[1]
Against the ground with bloody strokes, himself e'en
    there to rid;
Had been my heart of flint, it must have melted
    tho';
For in my life I never saw a man so full of woe.
With tears for his redress I rashly to him ran,
And in my arms I caught him fast, and thus I spake
    him than:
'What woful wight art thou, that in such heavy
    case
Torments thyself with such despite, here in this
    desart place?'
Wherewith as all aghast, fulfill'd with ire and dread,
He cast on me a staring look, with colour pale and
    dead:
'Nay, what art thou,' quoth he, 'that in this heavy
    plight

[1] Destroy.

Dost find me here, most woful wretch, that life hath
    in despite?'
'I am,' quoth I, 'but poor, and simple in degree;
A shepherd's charge I have in hand, unworthy
    though I be.'
With that he gave a sigh, as though the sky should
    fall,
And loud, alas! he shrieked oft, and, 'Shepherd,'
    gan he call,
'Come, hie thee fast at once, and print it in thy
    heart,
So thou shalt know, and I shall tell thee, guiltless
    how I smart.'
His back against the tree sore feebled all with faint,
With weary sprite he stretcht him up, and thus he
    told his plaint:
'Once in my heart,' quoth he, 'it chanced me to
    love
Such one, in whom hath Nature wrought, her cun-
    ning for to prove.
And sure I cannot say, but many years were spent,
With such good will so recompens'd, as both we
    were content.
Whereto then I me bound, and she likewise also,
The sun should run his course awry, ere we this faith
    forego.
Who joyed then but I? who had this worldès bliss?
Who might compare a life to mine, that never
    thought on this?
But dwelling in this truth, amid my greatest joy,

Is me befallen a greater loss than Priam had of Troy.
She is reversèd clean, and beareth me in hand,
That my deserts have given cause to break this
    faithful band:
And for my just excuse availeth no defence.
Now knowest thou all; I can no more; but, Shep-
    herd, hie thee hence,
And give him leave to die, that may no longer live:
Whose record, lo! I claim to have, my death I do
    forgive.
And eke when I am gone, be bold to speak it plain,
Thou hast seen die the truest man that ever love did
    pain.'
Wherewith he turned him round, and gasping oft
    for breath,
Into his arms a tree he raught, and said: ' Welcome
    my death!
Welcome a thousand fold, now dearer unto me
Than should, without her love to live, an emperor
    to be.'
Thus in this woful state he yielded up the ghost;
And little knoweth his lady, what a lover she hath
    lost.
Whose death when I beheld, no marvel was it, right
For pity though my heart did bleed, to see so piteous
    sight.
My blood from heat to cold oft changed wonders
    sore;
A thousand troubles there I found I never knew
    before;

'Tween dread and dolour so my sprites were brought
    in fear,
That long it was ere I could call to mind what I
    did there.
But as each thing hath end, so had these pains of
    mine:
The furies past, and I my wits restor'd by length of
    time.
Then as I could devise, to seek I thought it best
Where I might find some worthy place for such a
    corse to rest.
And in my mind it came, from thence not far away,
Where Cressid's love, king Priam's son, the worthy
    Troilus lay.
By him I made his tomb, in token he was true,
And as to him belonged well, I covered it with blue.
Whose soul by angels' power departed not so soon,
But to the heavens, lo! it fled, for to receive his
    doom.

COMPLAINT OF THE ABSENCE OF HER LOVER, BEING UPON THE SEA.

Good ladies! ye that have your pleasure in exile,
Step in your foot, come, take a place, and mourn
    with me awhile:
And such as by their lords do set but little price,
Let them sit still, it skills them not what chance
    come on the dice.

But ye whom Love hath bound, by order of de-
    sire,
To love your Lords, whose good deserts none other
    would require;
Come ye yet once again, and set your foot by mine,
Whose woful plight, and sorrows great, no tongue
    may well define.
My love and lord, alas! in whom consists my wealth,
Hath fortune sent to pass the seas, in hazard of his
    health.
Whom I was wont t'embrace with well contented
    mind,
Is now amid the foaming floods at pleasure of the
    wind.
Where God will him preserve, and soon him home
    me send;
Without which hope my life, alas! were shortly at
    an end.
Whose absence yet, although my hope doth tell
    me plain,
With short return he comes anon, yet ceaseth not
    my pain.
The fearful dreams I have ofttimes do grieve me so,
That when I wake, I lie in doubt, where they be
    true or no.
Sometime the roaring seas, me seems, do grow so
    high,
That my dear Lord, ay me! alas! methinks I see
    him die.
And other time the same, doth tell me he is come,

And playing, where I shall him find, with his fair
    little son.[1]
So forth I go apace to see that liefsome sight,
And with a kiss, methinks I say, 'Welcome, my
    Lord, my knight;
Welcome, my sweet; alas! the stay of my welfare;
Thy presence bringeth forth a truce betwixt me
    and my care.'
Then lively doth he look, and salueth me again,
And saith, ' My dear, how is it now that you have
    all this pain? '
Wherewith the heavy cares, that heap'd are in my
    breast,
Break forth and me dischargen clean, of all my huge
    unrest.
But when I me awake, and find it but a dream,
The anguish of my former woe beginneth more
    extreme;
And me tormenteth so that unneath[2] may I find
Some hidden place, wherein to slake the gnawing
    of my mind.

[1] In the copy printed by Dr. Nott from the Harrington MS.
this line stands,

    " And playing, where I shall him find with T. his little son; "

which induces that writer to observe: " This proves the piece
to have been written, not as an exercise of fancy, but for some
existing person." If this conjecture be correct, the Complainant
may have been intended for Lady Surrey, and " T. his little
son," for *Thomas* her eldest son, afterwards Duke of Norfolk.

    [2] With difficulty.

Thus every way you see, with absence how I burn;
And for my wound no cure I find, but hope of good
    return:
Save when I think, by sour how sweet is felt the
    more,
It doth abate some of my pains, that I abode before.
And then unto myself I say: 'When we shall meet,
But little while shall seem this pain; the joy shall
    be so sweet.'
Ye winds, I you conjure, in chiefest of your rage,
That ye my Lord me safely send, my sorrows to
    assuage.
And that I may not long abide in this excess,
Do your good will to cure a wight, that liveth in
    distress.

—◆—

A PRAISE OF HIS LOVE,

WHEREIN HE REPROVETH THEM THAT COMPARE THEIR
LADIES WITH HIS.

GIVE place, ye lovers, here before
That spent your boasts and brags in vain ;
My Lady's beauty passeth more
The best of yours, I dare well sayen,
Than doth the sun the candle light,
Or brightest day the darkest night.

And thereto hath a troth as just
As had Penelope the fair ;

For what she saith, ye may it trust,
As it by writing sealed were:
And virtues hath she many mo'
Than I with pen have skill to show.

I could rehearse, if that I would,
The whole effect of Nature's plaint,
When she had lost the perfect mould,
The like to whom she could not paint:
With wringing hands, how she did cry,
And what she said, I know it, aye.

I know she swore with raging mind,
Her kingdom only set apart,
There was no loss by law of kind
That could have gone so near her heart;
And this was chiefly all her pain;
'She could not make the like again.'

Sith Nature thus gave her the praise,
To be the chiefest work she wrought;
In faith, methink! some better ways
On your behalf might well be sought,
Than to compare, as ye have done,
To match the candle with the sun.

TO HIS MISTRESS.[1]

IF he that erst the form so lively drew
Of Venus' face, triumph'd in painter's art;
Thy Father then what glory did ensue,
By whose pencil a Goddess made thou art.
Touched with flame that figure made some rue,
And with her love surprised many a heart.
There lack'd yet that should cure their hot desire:
Thou canst inflame and quench the kindled fire.

———◆———

TO THE LADY THAT SCORNED HER LOVER.

ALTHOUGH I had a check,
To give the mate is hard;
For I have found a neck,
To keep my men in guard.
And you that hardy are,
To give so great assay
Unto a man of war,
To drive his men away;

[1] Printed for the first time by Dr. Nott, from a MS. in the possession of Mr. Hill.

I rede you take good heed,
And mark this foolish verse;
For I will so provide,
That I will have your ferse.[1]
And when your ferse is had,
And all your war is done;
Then shall yourself be glad
To end that you begun.

For if by chance I win
Your person in the field;
Too late then come you in
Yourself to me to yield.
For I will use my power,
As captain full of might;
And such I will devour,
As use to shew me spite.

And for because you gave
Me check in such degree;
This vantage, lo! I have,
Now check, and guard to thee.
Defend it if thou may;
Stand stiff in thine estate:
For sure I will assay,
If I can give thee mate.

[1] The Queen at Chess.

3

A WARNING TO THE LOVER, HOW HE IS
ABUSED BY HIS LOVE.

Too dearly had I bought my green and youthful
  years,
If in mine age I could not find when craft for love
  appears.
And seldom though I come in court among the rest,
Yet can I judge in colours dim, as deep as can the
  best.
Where grief torments the man that suff'reth secret
  smart,
To break it forth unto some friend, it easeth well
  the heart.
So stands it now with me, for, my beloved friend,
This case is thine, for whom I feel such torment of
  my mind.
And for thy sake I burn so in my secret breast,
That till thou know my whole disease, my heart can
  have no rest,
I see how thine abuse hath wrested so thy wits,
That all it yields to thy desire, and follows thee by
  fits.
Where thou hast loved so long, with heart, and all
  thy power,
I see thee fed with feigned words, thy freedom to
  devour:

I know (though she say nay, and would it well
    withstand)   [but in hand.
When in her grace thou held thee most, she bare thee
I see her pleasant chere in chiefest of thy suit;
When thou art gone, I see him come that gathers
    up the fruit.
And eke in thy respect, I see the base degree
Of him to whom she gave the heart, that promised
    was to thee.   [sure
I see, (what would you more,) stood never man so
On woman's word, but wisdom would mistrust it to
    endure.

—◆—

THE FORSAKEN LOVER DESCRIBETH AND FORSAKETH LOVE.

O LOATHSOME place! where I
Have seen, and heard my dear;
When in my heart her eye
Hath made her thought appear,
 By glimpsing with such grace, —
As fortune it ne would
That lasten any space,
Between us longer should.

As fortune did advance
To further my desire;
Even so hath fortune's chance
Thrown all amidst the mire.

And that I have deserved,
With true and faithful heart,
Is to his hands reserved,
That never felt the smart.

But happy is that man
That scaped hath the grief,
That love well teach him can,
By wanting his relief.
A scourge to quiet minds
It is, who taketh heed;
A common plage that binds;
A travail without meed.

This gift it hath also:
Whoso enjoys it most,
A thousand troubles grow,
To vex his wearied ghost.
And last it may not long;
The truest thing of all:
And sure the greatest wrong,
That is within this thrall.

But since thou, desert place,
Canst give me no account
Of my desired grace,
That I to have was wont;
Farewell! thou hast me taught,
To think me not the first
That love hath set aloft,
And casten in the dust.

THE LOVER DESCRIBETH HIS RESTLESS STATE.[1]

As oft as I behold, and see
The sovereign beauty that me bound;
The nigher my comfort is to me,
Alas! the fresher is my wound.

As flame doth quench by rage of fire,
And running streams consume by rain;
So doth the sight that I desire
Appease my grief, and deadly pain.

Like as the fly that see'th the flame,
And thinks to play her in the fire;
That found her woe, and sought her game
Where grief did grow by her desire.

First when I saw those crystal streams,
Whose beauty made my mortal wound;
I little thought within their beams
So sweet a venom to have found.

---

1 The 3rd, 6th, and 8th stanzas do not occur in Tottel's collection, but were supplied by Dr. Nott from a copy in the " Nugæ Antiquæ."

But wilful will did prick me forth,
Blind Cupid did me whip and guide;
Force made me take my grief in worth; [1]
My fruitless hope my harm did hide;

Wherein is hid the cruel bit,
Whose sharp repulse none can resist;
And eke the spur that strains each wit
To run the race against his list.

As cruel waves full oft be found
Against the rocks to roar and cry;
So doth my heart full oft rebound
Against my breast full bitterly.

And as the spider draws her line,
With labour lost I frame my suit;
The fault is her's, the loss is mine:
Of ill sown seed, such is the fruit.

I fall, and see mine own decay;
As he that bears flame in his breast,
Forgets for pain to cast away
The thing that breedeth his unrest. [2]

---

[1] Patiently.
[2] In Tottel's collection this stanza is thus printed —

> I fall and see mine own decay,
> As one that bears flame in his breast;
> Forgets in pain to put away
> The thing that breedeth mine unrest.

THE LOVER EXCUSETH HIMSELF OF
SUSPECTED CHANGE.

THOUGH I regarded not
The promise made by me;
Or passed not to spot
My faith and honesty:
Yet were my fancy strange,
And wilful will to wite,
If I sought now to change
A falcon for a kite.

All men might well dispraise
My wit and enterprise,
If I esteemed a pese [1]
Above a pearl in price:
Or judged the owl in sight
The sparhawk to excel;
Which flieth but in the night,
As all men know right well.

Or if I sought to sail
Into the brittle port,
Where anchor hold doth fail
To such as do resort;

[1] A pea.

And leave the haven sure,
Where blows no blustering wind;
No fickleness in ure,[1]
So far-forth as I find.

No! think me not so light,
Nor of so churlish kind,
Though it lay in my might
My bondage to unbind,
That I would leave the hind
To hunt the gander's foe.
No! no! I have no mind
To make exchanges so.

Nor yet to change at all;
For think, it may not be
That I should seek to fall
From my felicity.
Desirous for to win,
And loth for to forego;
Or new change to begin;
How may all this be so?

The fire it cannot freeze,
For it is not his kind;
Nor true love cannot lese
The constance of the mind.
Yet as soon shall the fire
Want heat to blaze and burn;
As I, in such desire,
Have once a thought to turn.

1 Practise.

A CARELESS MAN

SCORNING AND DESCRIBING THE SUBTLE USAGE OF WOMEN
TOWARD THEIR LOVERS.

WRATP in my careless cloak, as I walk to and fro,
I see how love can shew what force there reigneth
     in his bow:
And how he shooteth eke a hardy heart to wound;
And where he glanceth by again, that little hurt is
     found.
For seldom is it seen he woundeth hearts alike;
The one may rage, when t'other's love is often far
     to seek.
All this I see, with more; and wonder thinketh me
How he can strike the one so sore, and leave the
     other free.
I see that wounded wight that suff'reth all this
     wrong,
How he is fed with yeas and nays, and liveth all
     too long.
In silence though I keep such secrets to myself,
Yet do I see how she sometime doth yield a look
     by stealth,
As though it seem'd; 'I wis, I will not lose thee so:'
When in her heart so sweet a thought did never
     truly grow.

Then say I thus: ' Alas! that man is far from bliss,
That doth receive for his relief none other gain but
    this.'
And she that feeds him so, I feel and find it plain,
Is but to glory in her power, that over such can
    reign.
Nor are such graces spent, but when she thinks
    that he,
A wearied man, is fully bent such fancies to let flee.
Then to retain him still, she wrasteth new her grace,
And smileth, lo! as though she would forthwith the
    man embrace.
But when the proof is made, to try such looks
    withal,
He findeth then the place all void, and freighted
    full of gall.
Lord! what abuse is this; who can such women
    praise?
That for their glory do devise to use such crafty
    ways.
I that among the rest do sit and mark the row,
Find that in her is greater craft, than is in twenty
    mo':
Whose tender years, alas! with wiles so well are
    sped,
What will she do when hoary hairs are powder'd in
    her head?

AN ANSWER IN THE BEHALF OF A WOMAN.

OF AN UNCERTAIN AUTHOR.[1]

GIRT in my guiltless gown, as I sit here and sow,
I see that things are not in deed, as to the outward
    show.
And who so list to look and note things somewhat
    near,
Shall find where plainness seems to haunt, nothing
    but craft appear.
For with indifferent eyes, myself can well discern,
How some to guide a ship in storms stick not[2] to
    take the stern;
Whose skill and courage tried[3] in calm to steer
    a barge,
They would soon shew, you should foresee,[4] it were
    too great a charge.
And some I see again sit still and say but small,
That can[5] do ten times more than they that say
    they can do all.

---

[1] This poem was printed as in the text by Dr. Nott, from the Harrington MS., which alone contains the last eighteen lines. The variations between that copy and the printed editions are pointed out in the notes. The remark in Tottel's Collection that it was by "an uncertain author" justifies a doubt whether it was written by Surrey.

[2] seek for.   [3] Whose practice if were proved.
[4] Assuredly believe it well.   [5] could.

Whose goodly gifts are such, the more they un-
    derstand,
The more they seek to learn and know, and take
    less charge in hand.
And to declare more plain, the time flits not so
    fast,
But I can bear right [1] well in mind the song now
    sung, and past;
The author whereof came, wrapt in a crafty cloak,
In [2] will to force a flaming fire where he could
    raise no smoke.
If power and will had met, [3] as it appeareth plain,
The [4] truth nor right had ta'en no place; their
    virtues had been vain.
So that you may perceive, and I may safely see,
The innocent that guiltless is, condemned should
    have be.
Much like untruth to this the story doth declare,
Where the Elders laid to Susan's charge meet
    matter to compare.
They did her both accuse, and eke condemn her too,
And yet no reason, right, nor truth, did lead them
    so to do!
And she thus judg'd to die, toward her death went
    forth,
Fraughted with faith, a patient pace, taking her
    wrong in worth.
But he that doth defend all those that in him trust,

---

[1] full.   [2] With.   [3] join'd.   [4] Then.

Did raise a child for her defence to shield her from
    th' unjust.
And Daniel chosen was then of this wrong to weet,
How, in what place, and eke with whom she did
    this crime commit.
He caused the Elders part the one from th' other's
    sight,
And did examine one by one, and charg'd them
    both say right.
'Under a mulberry tree it was;' first said the one.
The next named a pomegranate tree, whereby the
    truth was known.
Then Susan was discharg'd, and they condemn'd
    to die,
As right requir'd, and they deserv'd, that fram'd so
    foul a lie.
And He that her preserv'd, and lett them of their
    lust,
Hath me defended hitherto, and will do still I trust.

THE CONSTANT LOVER LAMENTETH.

SINCE fortune's wrath envieth the wealth
Wherein I reigned, by the sight
Of that, that fed mine eyes by stealth
With sour, sweet, dread, and delight;
Let not my grief move you to moan,
For I will weep and wail alone.

Spite drave me into Boreas' reign,
Where hoary frosts the fruits do bite,
When hills were spread, and every plain
With stormy winter's mantle white;
And yet, my dear, such was my heat,
When others froze, then did I sweat.

And now, though on the sun I drive,
Whose fervent flame all things decays;
His beams in brightness may not strive
With light of your sweet golden rays;
Nor from my breast his heat remove
The frozen thoughts, graven by Love.

Ne may the waves of the salt flood
Quench that your beauty set on fire;
For though mine eyes forbear the food,
That did relieve the hot desire;
Such as I was, such will I be;
Your own; what would ye more of me?

A SONG WRITTEN BY THE EARL OF SURREY

OF A LADY THAT REFUSED TO DANCE WITH HIM.[1]

EACH beast can choose his fere according to his
    mind,
And eke can shew a friendly chere, like to their
    beastly kind.
A Lion saw I late, as white as any snow,
Which seemed well to lead the race, his port the
    same did show.
Upon the gentle beast to gaze it pleased me,
For still me thought he seemed well of noble blood
    to be.

1 Dr. Nott's remark on this piece, "That it is valuable from
the circumstance of its preserving an account of a quarrel between Surrey and the fair Geraldine, which, as we hear nothing
of any reconciliation afterwards, was the occasion probably
of his renouncing his ill fated passion," is an amusing instance
of first imagining a fact, and then making every circumstance
support it. The learned editor, as in most other instances,
assumes that Geraldine was the subject of the poem, without
a shadow of evidence; and gratuitously gives it this title —
" Surrey renounces all affection for the fair Geraldine," whereas,
in all the printed editions, it bears the title assigned to·it in
the text. There is no doubt that Surrey personated himself
by the " White Lion," which was one of the badges (and not
the arms, as Dr. Nott asserts) of the house of Howard, derived
from their descent from the Mowbrays, Dukes of Norfolk. The
word " pranceth " in line 7, alluded to the position " rampant"

And as he pranced before, still seeking for a make,
As who would say, 'There is none here, I trow,
    will me forsake.'
I might perceive a Wolf as white as whalèsbone;
A fairer beast of fresher hue, beheld I never none;
Save that her looks were coy, and froward eke her
    grace:
Unto the which this gentle beast gan him advance
    apace.
And with a beck full low he bowed at her feet,
In humble wise, as who would say, 'I am too far
    unmeet.'
But such a scornful chere, wherewith she him re-
    warded!
Was never seen, I trow, the like, to such as well
    deserved.

of the animal, and perhaps a playful reference was intended to
Surrey's invitation to the lady to *dance*. But there is not any
reason to presume by the *Wolf* the fair Geraldine was intended,
though it is almost certain that the family of the lady adverted to
bore that animal on their standards, or in their arms. Dr. Nott has
cited a MS. in the Museum to prove that the Fitzgeralds, Earls
of Kildare, used a Wolf as their crest, but this is unsupported
by any other authority, and Drayton, with more probability,
says, that the lady meant by the "Wolf," was Ann, the daughter
of Sir Edward Stanhope, who became the wife of the Protector
Somerset. The Stanhope family once used a Wolf as their
crest, in consequence of their descent from Maulovel, and a
Wolf is still one of the supporters of the Earls of Chesterfield,
Stanhope, and Harrington. See Collins' Peerage, Ed. 1779, iii.
301, 302. It is proper to add, that the family of Arundell of Lan-
hearne, in Cornwall, bore a white wolf as a badge.

With that she start aside well near a foot or twain,

And unto him thus gan she say, with spite and
    great disdain :

' Lion,' she said, ' if thou hadst known my mind
    before,

Thou hadst not spent thy travail thus, nor all thy
    pain for-lore.

Do way! I let thee weet, thou shalt not play with
    me :

Go range about, where thou mayst find some
    meeter fere for thee.'

With that he beat his tail, his eyes began to flame ;

I might perceive his noble heart much moved by
    the same.

Yet saw I him refrain, and eke his wrath assuage,

And unto her thus gan he say, when he was past
    his rage :

' Cruel! you do me wrong, to set me thus so light ;

Without desert for my good will to shew me such
    despite.

How can ye thus intreat a Lion of the race,

That with his paws a crowned king devoured in the
    place.[1]

Whose nature is to prey upon no simple food,

As long as he may suck the flesh, and drink of
    noble blood.

---

[1] Apparently an allusion to the defeat and death of James the
Fourth at Flodden Field, by Thomas, then Earl of Surrey, the
Poet's grandfather.

4

If you be fair and fresh, am I not of your hue ? [1]
And for my vaunt I dare well say, my blood is not
    untrue.
For you yourself have heard, it is not long ago,
Sith that for love one of the race did end his life in
    woe,
In tower both strong and high, for his assured truth,
Whereas in tears he spent his breath, alas! the
    more the ruth.
This gentle beast so died, whom nothing could
    remove,
But willingly to lese his life for loss of his true
    love.[2]

[1] Query, is it to be understood by this line that Surrey was
related to the lady, or did he only mean that his lion was of the
same hue as her wolf?

[2] Dr. Nott observes: " This means Thomas Howard, second
son of Thomas second Duke of Norfolk, by Agnes his second
wife, and consequently half uncle to Surrey. He was attainted
of high treason, and committed to the Tower, in June, 1536, for
having, without the knowledge or approbation of King Henry
VIII., affianced himself to the Lady Margaret Douglas, daughter
of Margaret Queen of Scotland, the King's sister. Lord Thomas
Howard remained in confinement till his decease on Allhallows
Eve, 1538. Upon his death the Lady Margaret, who had been
confined likewise, was set at liberty. It is probable that this
unfortunate affiance was the effect on the part of Lord Thomas
Howard, as well as on the part of the Lady Margaret, of real
attachment, and not of ambition. Had he relinquished all claim
to her hand, he probably would have been released from his confinement. It is likely therefore that his love, as Surrey inti-
mates, really cost him his life."

Other there be whose lives do linger still in pain,
Against their will preserved are, that would have
      died fain.
But now I do perceive that nought it moveth you,
My good intent, my gentle heart, nor yet my kind
      so true.
But that your will is such to lure me to the trade,
As other some full many years trace by the craft ye
      made.
And thus behold my kinds, how that we differ far;
I seek my foes; and you your friends do threaten
      still with war.
I fawn where I am fled; you slay, that seeks to
      you;
I can devour no yielding prey; you kill where you
      subdue.
My kind is to desire the honour of the field;
And you with blood to slake your thirst on such as
      to you yield.
Wherefore I would you wist, that for your coyed
      looks,
I am no man that will be trapp'd, nor tangled with
      such hooks.
And though some lust to love, where blame full well
      they might;
And to such beasts of current sought, that should
      have travail bright;
I will observe the law that Nature gave to me,
To conquer such as will resist, and let the rest go
      free.

And as a falcon free, that soareth in the air,
Which never fed on hand nor lure; nor for no
stale [1] doth care;
While that I live and breathe, such shall my cus-
tom be
In wildness of the woods to seek my prey, where
pleaseth me;
Where many one shall rue, that never made offence:
Thus your refuse against my power shall boot them
no defence.
And for revenge thereof I vow and swear thereto,
A thousand spoils I shall commit I never thought
to do.
And if to light on you my luck so good shall be,
I shall be glad to feed on that, that would have fed
on me.   [bow;
And thus farewell, Unkind, to whom I bent and
I would you wist, the ship is safe that bare his sails
so low.
Sith that a Lion's heart is for a Wolf no prey,
With bloody mouth go slake your thirst on simple
sheep, I say,
With more despite and ire than I can now express;
Which to my pain, though I refrain, the cause you
may well guess.
As for because myself was author of the game,
It boots me not that for my wrath I should disturb
the same.'

[1] A piece of meat used to allure falcons back to their master.

THE FAITHFUL LOVER

DECLARETH HIS PAINS AND HIS UNCERTAIN JOYS, AND
WITH ONLY HOPE RECOMFORTETH SOMEWHAT
HIS WOFUL HEART.

IF care do cause men cry, why do not I complain?
If each man do bewail his woe, why shew not I my
  pain?
Since that amongst them all, I dare well say is
  none
So far from weal, so full of woe, or hath more cause
  to moan.
For all things having life, sometime hath quiet rest;
The bearing ass, the drawing ox, and every other
  beast;
The peasant, and the post, that serves at all assays;
The ship-boy, and the galley-slave, have time to
  take their ease;
Save I, alas! whom care, of force doth so constrain,
To wail the day, and wake the night, continually in
  pain.
From pensiveness to plaint, from plaint to bitter
  tears,
From tears to painful plaint again; and thus my
  life it wears.
No thing under the sun, that I can hear or see,
But moveth me for to bewail my cruel destiny.

For where men do rejoice, since that I cannot so,
I take no pleasure in that place, it doubleth but my
    woe.
And when I hear the sound of song or instrument,
Methink each tune there doleful is, and helps me to
    lament.
And if I see some have their most desired sight,
'Alas!' think I, 'each man hath weal save I, most
    woful wight.'
Then as the stricken deer withdraws himself alone,
So do I seek some secret place, where I may make
    my moan.
There do my flowing eyes shew forth my melting
    heart;
So that the streams of those two wells right well de-
    clare my smart.
And in those cares so cold, I force myself a heat
(As sick men in their shaking fits procure them-
    selves to sweat)
With thoughts, that for the time do much appease
    my pain:
But yet they cause a farther fear, and breed my
    woe again.
Methink within my thought I see right plain appear
My heart's delight, my sorrow's leech, mine earthly
    goddess here,
With every sundry grace, that I have seen her have:
Thus I within my woful breast her picture paint
    and grave.

And in my thought I roll her beauties to and fro;
Her laughing chere, her lively look, my heart that
    pierced so.
Her strangeness when I sued her servant for to be;
And what she said, and how she smiled, when that
    she pitied me.
Then comes a sudden fear that reaveth all my rest,
Lest absence cause forgetfulness to sink within her
    breast.
For when I think how far this earth doth us divide,
Alas! me-seems love throws me down; I feel how
    that I slide.   [trust
But then I think again, ' Why should I thus mis-
So sweet a wight, so sad and wise, that is so true and
    just?
For loath she was to love, and wavering is she not;
The farther off the more desired.' Thus lovers tie
    their knot.
So in despair and hope plung'd am I both up and
    down,
As is the ship with wind and wave, when Neptune
    list to frown:
But as the watery showers delay the raging wind,
So doth Good-hope clean put away despair out of
    my mind;
And bids me for to serve, and suffer patiently:
For what wot I the after weal that fortune wills to
    me.
For those that care do know, and tasted have of
    trouble,

When passed is their woful pain, each joy shall
    seem them double.
And bitter sends she now, to make me taste the
    better
The pleasant sweet, when that it comes, to make it
    seem the sweeter.
And so determine I to serve until my breath;
Yea, rather die a thousand times, than once to false
    my faith.
And if my feeble corpse, through weight of woful
    smart
Do fail, or faint, my will it is that still she keep my
    heart.
And when this carcass here to earth shall be refar'd,
I do bequeath my wearied ghost to serve her after-
    ward.

THE MEANS TO ATTAIN HAPPY LIFE.

MARTIAL, the things that do attain
The happy life, be these, I find:
The riches left, not got with pain;
The fruitful ground, the quiet mind:

The equal friend, no grudge, no strife;
No charge of rule, nor governance;
Without disease, the healthful life;
The household of continuance:

The mean diet, no delicate fare;
True wisdom join'd with simpleness;
The night discharged of all care,
Where wine the wit may not oppress:

The faithful wife, without debate;
Such sleeps as may beguile the night.
Contented with thine own estate;
Ne wish for Death, ne fear his might.

PRAISE OF MEAN AND CONSTANT ESTATE

OF thy life, Thomas,[1] this compass well mark :
Not aye with full sails the high seas to beat ;
Ne by coward dread, in shunning storms dark,
On shallow shores thy keel in peril freat.

Whoso gladly halseth [2] the golden mean,
Void of dangers advisedly hath his home ;
Not with loathsome muck as a den unclean,
Nor palace like, whereat disdain may glome.[8]

The lofty pine the great wind often rives ;
With violenter sway fallen turrets steep ;
Lightnings assault the high mountains and clives.[4]
A heart well stay'd, in overthwartes [5] deep.

Hopeth amends ; in sweet, doth fear the sour.
God that sendeth, withdraweth winter sharp.
Now ill, not aye thus ; once Phœbus to low'r,
With bow unbent, shall cease ; and frame to harp.

His voice in strait estate appear thou stout ;
And so wisely, when lucky gale of wind
All thy puft sails shall fill, look well about ;
Take in a reef : haste is waste, proof doth find.

[1] Sir Thomas Wyatt.   [2] Embraceth.
[8] Look at scornfully.   [4] Steep cliffs.
[5] Adverse fortunes.

PRAISE OF CERTAIN PSALMS OF DAVID.

TRANSLATED BY SIR THOMAS [WYATT] THE ELDER.

THE great Macedon, that out of Persia chased
Darius, of whose huge power all Asia rung;
In the rich ark Dan Homer's rhymes he placed,
Who feigned gests of heathen princes sung.
What holy grave, what worthy sepulture,
To Wyatt's Psalms should Christians then pur-
          chase?
Where he doth paint the lively faith, and pure,
The steadfast hope, the sweet return to grace,
Of just David, by perfect penitence;
Where Rulers may see in a mirror clear,
The bitter fruit of false concupiscence;
How Jewry bought Urias' death full dear.
      In Princes' hearts God's scourge imprinted deep,
      Ought them awake out of their sinful sleep.

----◆----

OF THE DEATH OF SIR THOMAS WYATT.

DIVERS thy death do diversely bemoan:
Some, that in presence of thy livelihed
Lurked, whose breasts envy with hate had swoln,
Yield Cæsar's tears upon Pompeius' head.

Some, that watched with the murd'rer's knife,
With eager thirst to drink thy guiltless blood,
Whose practice brake by happy end of life,
With envious tears to hear thy fame so good.
But I, that knew what harbour'd in that head;
What virtues rare were tempered in that breast;
Honour the place that such a jewel bred,
And kiss the ground whereas the corpse doth rest;
   With vapour'd eyes: from whence such streams
      availe,[1]
As Pyramus did on Thisbe's breast bewail.

——◆——

OF THE SAME.

WYATT resteth here, that quick could never rest:
Whose heavenly gifts increased by disdain;
And virtue sank the deeper in his breast:
Such profit he by envy could obtain.
A head, where wisdom mysteries did frame;
Whose hammers beat still in that lively brain,
As on a stithe,[2] where that some work of fame
Was daily wrought, to turn to Britain's gain.
A visage stern, and mild; where both did grow
Vice to contemn, in virtue to rejoice:
Amid great storms, whom grace assured so,
To live upright, and smile at fortune's choice.

---

[1] Fall down.   [2] Forge, or anvil.

A hand, that taught what might be said in rhyme;
That reft Chaucer the glory of his wit.
A mark, the which (unperfected for time)
Some may approach, but never none shall hit.
A tongue that serv'd in foreign realms his king;
Whose courteous talk to virtue did inflame
Each noble heart; a worthy guide to bring
Our English youth by travail unto fame.
An eye, whose judgment none effect could blind,
Friends to allure, and foes to reconcile;
Whose piercing look did represent a mind
With virtue fraught, reposed, void of guile.
A heart, where dread was never so imprest
To hide the thought that might the truth advance;
In neither fortune loft, nor yet represt,
To swell in wealth, or yield unto mischance.
A valiant corpse, where force and beauty met:
Happy, alas! too happy, but for foes,
Lived, and ran the race that nature set;
Of manhood's shape, where she the mould did lose.
But to the heavens that simple soul is fled,
Which left, with such as covet Christ to know,
Witness of faith, that never shall be dead;
Sent for our health, but not received so.
Thus for our guilt this jewel have we lost;
The earth his bones, the heavens possess his ghost.

OF THE SAME.

In the rude age, when knowledge was not rife,
If Jove in Crete, and other were that taught
Arts, to convert to profit of our life,
Wend after death to have their temples sought:
If, Virtue yet no void unthankful time
Failed of some to blast her endless fame;
(A goodly mean both to deter from crime,
And to her steps our sequel to inflame)
In days of truth if Wyatt's friends then wail
(The only debt that dead of quick may claim)
That rare wit spent, employ'd to our avail,
Where Christ is taught, we led to Virtue's train.
   His lively face their breasts how did it freat,
   Whose cinders yet with envy they do eat.

—◆—

AN EPITAPH ON CLERE, SURREY'S FAITHFUL FRIEND AND FOLLOWER.

NORFOLK sprung thee, Lambeth holds thee dead;
Clere, of the Count of Cleremont, thou hight [1]
Within the womb of Ormond's race thou bred,
And saw'st thy cousin crowned in thy sight.

[1] These lines were inscribed, with the epitaph above, on a table
in Lambeth Church:—
"Epitaphium Thomæ Clere, qui fato functus est 1545 auctore

Shelton for love, Surrey for lord thou chase;[1]
(Aye, me! whilst life did last that league was tender)
Tracing whose steps thou sawest Kelsal blaze,
Landrecy burnt, and batter'd Boulogne render.
At Montreuil gates, hopeless of all recure,
Thine Earl, half dead, gave in thy hand his will;
Which cause did thee this pining death procure,
Ere summers four times seven thou couldst fulfill.
Ah! Clere! if love had booted, care, or cost,
Heaven had not won, nor earth so timely lost.

Henrico Howard, Comite Surrey. In cujus faelicis ingenii specimen, et singularis facundiae argumentum, appensa fuit haec Tabula per W. Howard, filium Thomae nuper Ducis Norfolciensis, filii ejusdem Henrici Comitis."

This epitaph occurs, with some trifling variations, in Camden's *Remains*, Aubrey's *History of Surrey*, v. 247, and in Bloomfield's *Norfolk*. Thomas Clere was the youngest son of Sir Robert Clere, of Ormesby in Norfolk, (the descendant of Clere, of Cleremont in Normandy,) by Alice, daughter of Sir William Boleyn, by Margaret, daughter and coheir of Thomas Boteler, Earl of Ormond. He was consequently first "cousin" of Queen Anne Boleyn, whom "he saw crowned" in 1533, and was connected with "Ormond's race." "Shelton" is presumed to have been a daughter of Sir John Shelton, of Shelton in Norfolk, but it does not appear that Clere married her. He died on the 14th of April, 1545, and was buried at Lambeth. These facts explain most of the allusions in the epitaph, and the others are noticed in the Memoir of Surrey.

[1] Didst choose.

OF SARDANAPALUS'S DISHONORABLE LIFE AND MISERABLE DEATH.

Th' Assyrian king, in peace, with foul desire
And filthy lusts that stain'd his regal heart;
In war, that should set princely hearts on fire,
Did yield vanquisht for want of martial art.
The dint of swords from kisses seemed strange;
And harder than his lady's side, his targe: [1]
From glutton feasts to soldier's fare, a change;
His helmet, far above a garland's charge:
Who scarce the name of manhood did retain,
Drenched in sloth and womanish delight.
Feeble of spirit, impatient of pain,
When he had lost his honour, and his right,
  (Proud time of wealth, in storms appalled with
     dread,)
  Murder'd himself, to shew some manful deed.

[1] Shield.

HOW NO AGE IS CONTENT

WITH HIS OWN ESTATE, AND HOW THE AGE OF CHILDREN
IS THE HAPPIEST IF THEY HAD SKILL
TO UNDERSTAND IT.

LAID in my quiet bed, in study as I were,
I saw within my troubled head a heap of thoughts
    appear.
And every thought did shew so lively in mine eyes,
That now I sigh'd, and then I smiled, as cause of
    thought did rise.
I saw the little boy in thought how oft that he
Did wish of God to scape the rod, a tall young man
    to be.
The young man eke that feels his bones with pains
    opprest,
How he would be a rich old man, to live and lie at
    rest.
The rich old man that sees his end draw on so sore,
How he would be a boy again, to live so much the
    more.
Whereat full oft I smiled, to see how all these three,
From boy to man, from man to boy, would chop
    and change degree.
And musing thus I think, the case is very strange,
That man from wealth, to live in woe, doth ever
    seek to change.

5

Thus thoughtful as I lay, I saw my wither'd skin,
How it doth shew my dented chews, the flesh was
    worn so thin.
And eke my toothless chaps, the gates of my right
    way,
That opes and shuts as I do speak, do thus unto me
    say :
' Thy white and hoarish airs, the messengers of age,
That shew, like lines of true belief, that this life
    doth assuage ;
Bid thee lay hand, and feel them hanging on thy
    chin ;
The which do write two ages past, the third now
    coming in.
Hang up therefore the bit of thy young wanton time :
And thou that therein beaten art, the happiest life
    define.'
Whereat I sigh'd, and said : ' Farewell ! my wonted
    joy ;
Truss up thy pack, and trudge from me to every
    little boy ;
And tell them thus from me ; their time most happy
    is,
If, to their time, they reason had, to know the truth
    of this.'

BONUM EST MIHI QUOD HUMILIASTI ME.

THE storms are past; the clouds are overblown;
And humble chere great rigour hath represt.
For the default is set a pain foreknown;
And patience graft in a determined breast.
And in the heart, where heaps of griefs were grown,
The sweet revenge hath planted mirth and rest.
No company so pleasant as mine own.

. . . .

Thraldom at large hath made this prison free.
Danger well past, remembered, works delight.
Of ling'ring doubts such hope is sprung, pardie!
That nought I find displeasant in my sight,
But when my glass presented unto me
The cureless wound that bleedeth day and night.
To think, alas! such hap should granted be
Unto a wretch, that hath no heart to fight,
To spill that blood, that hath so oft been shed,
For Britain's sake, alas! and now is dead!

EXHORTATION TO LEARN BY OTHERS' TROUBLE.

My Ratclif,[1] when thy rechless [2] youth offends,
Receive thy scourge by others' chastisement;
For such calling, when it works none amends,
Then plagues are sent without advertisement.
Yet Solomon said, the wronged shall recure:
But Wyatt said true; 'The scar doth aye endure.'

THE FANCY OF A WEARIER LOVER.

The fancy, which that I have served long;
That hath alway been enemy to mine ease;
Seemed of late to rue upon my wrong,
And bade me fly the cause of my misease.
And I forthwith did press out of the throng,
That thought by flight my painful heart to please
Some other way, till I saw faith more strong;
And to myself I said, ' Alas ! those days

---

1 Perhaps Sir Humphrey Ratcliffe, one of the gentlemen pen-
sioners.
2 Careless.

In vain were spent, to run the race so long.'
And with that thought I met my guide, that plain,
Out of the way wherein I wander'd wrong,
Brought me amidst the hills in base Bullayne:
  Where I am now, as restless to remain
  Against my will, full pleased with my pain.

A SATIRE AGAINST THE CITIZENS OF LONDON.

    LONDON! hast thou accused me
    Of breach of laws? the root of strife!
    Within whose breast did boil to see,
    So fervent hot, thy dissolute life;
    That even the hate of sins, that grow
    Within thy wicked walls so rife,
    For to break forth did convert so,
    That terror could it not repress.
    The which, by words, since preachers know
    What hope is left for to redress,
    By unknown means it liked me
    My hidden burthen to express.
    Whereby it might appear to thee
    That secret sin hath secret spite;
    From justice' rod no fault is free
    But that all such as work unright
    In most quiet, are next ill rest.
    In secret silence of the night

This made me, with a rechless breast,
To wake thy sluggards with my bow:
A figure of the Lord's behest;
Whose scourge for sin the Scriptures shew.
That as the fearful thunder's clap
By sudden flame at hand we know;
Of pebble stones the soundless rap,
The dreadful plague might make thee see
Of God's wrath, that doth thee enwrap.
That pride might know, from conscience free,
How lofty works may her defend;
And envy find, as he hath sought,
How other seek him to offend:
And wrath taste of each cruel thought,
The just shape higher in the end:
And idle sloth, that never wrought,
To heaven his spirit lift may begin:
And greedy lucre live in dread,
To see what hate ill got goods win.
The lechers, ye that lusts do feed,
Perceive what secrecy is in sin:
And gluttons' hearts for sorrow bleed,
Awaked, when their fault they find,
In loathsome vice each drunken wight,
To stir to God this was my mind.
Thy windows had done me no spight;
But proud people that dread no fall,
Clothed with falsehood, and unright
Bred in the closures of thy wall.
But wrested to wrath in fervent zeal

Thou hast to strife, my secret call.
Indured hearts no warning feel.
O! shameless whore! is dread then gone?
Be such thy foes, as mean thy weal?
O! member of false Babylon!
The shop of craft! the den of ire!
Thy dreadful doom draws fast upon.
Thy martyr's blood by sword and fire,
In heaven and earth for justice call.
The Lord shall hear their just desire!
The flame of wrath shall on thee fall!
With famine and pest lamentably
Stricken shall be thy lechers all.
Thy proud towers, and turrets high
Enemies to God, beat stone from stone:
Thine idols burnt that wrought iniquity:
When, none thy ruin shall bemoan;
But render unto the righteous Lord,
That so hath judged Babylon,
Immortal praise with one accord.

----&----

A DESCRIPTION OF THE RESTLESS STATE

OF THE LOVER WHEN ABSENT FROM THE MISTRESS OF HIS HEART.

THE Sun, when he hath spread his rays,
And shewed his face ten thousand ways;
Ten thousand things do then begin,
To shew the life that they are in.

The heaven shews lively art and hue,
Of sundry shapes and colours new,
And laughs upon the earth; anon,
The earth, as cold as any stone,
Wet in the tears of her own kind,
'Gins then to take a joyful mind.
For well she feels that out and out
The sun doth warm her round about,
And dries her children tenderly;
And shews them forth full orderly.
The mountains high, and how they stand!
The valleys, and the great main land!
The trees, the herbs, the towers strong,
The castles, and the rivers long!
And even for joy thus of this heat
She sheweth forth her pleasures great,
And sleeps no more; but sendeth forth
Her clergions,[1] her own dear worth,
To mount and fly up to the air;
Where then they sing in order fair,
And tell in song full merrily,
How they have slept full quietly
That night, about their mother's sides.
And when they have sung more besides,
Then fall they to their mother's breast,
Whereas they feed, or take their rest.
The hunter then sounds out his horn,
And rangeth straight through wood and corn.

[1] Young brood.

On hills then shew the ewe and lamb,
And every young one with his dam.
Then lovers walk and tell their tale,
Both of their bliss, and of their bale;
And how they serve, and how they do,
And how their lady loves them too.
Then tune the birds their harmony;
Then flock the fowl in company;
Then every thing doth pleasure find
In that, that comforts all their kind.
No dreams do drench them of the night
Of foes, that would them slay, or bite,
As hounds, to hunt them at the tail;
Or men force them through hill and dale.
The sheep then dreams not of the wolf:
The shipman forces not the gulf;
The lamb thinks not the butcher's knife
Should then bereave him of his life.
For when the sun doth once run in,
Then all their gladness doth begin;
And then their skips, and then their play:
So falls their sadness then away.
    And thus all things have comforting
In that, that doth them comfort bring;
Save I, alas! whom neither sun,
Nor aught that God hath wrought and done
May comfort aught; as though I were
A thing not made for comfort here.
For being absent from your sight,
Which are my joy and whole delight,

My comfort, and my pleasure too,
How can I joy! how should I do?
May sick men laugh, that roar for pain?
Joy they in song, that do complain?
Are martyrs in their torments glad?
Do pleasures please them that are mad?
Then how may I in comfort be,
That lack the thing should comfort me?
The blind man oft, that lacks his sight,
Complains not most the lack of light;
But those that knew their perfectness,
And then do miss their blissfulness,
In martyr's tunes they sing, and wail
The want of that, which doth them fail.

And hereof comes that in my brains
So many fancies work my pains.
For when I weigh your worthiness,
Your wisdom, and your gentleness,
Your virtues and your sundry grace,
And mind the countenance of your face;
And how that you are she alone,
To whom I must both plain and moan;
Whom I do love, and must do still;
Whom I embrace, and aye so will,
To serve and please eke as I can,
As may a woful faithful man;
And find myself so far you fro,
God knows, what torment and what woe,
My rueful heart doth then embrace;
The blood then changeth in my face;

My sinews dull, in dumps [1] I stand,
No life I feel in foot nor hand,
As pale as any clout, and dead.
Lo! suddenly the blood o'erspread,
And gone again, it nill so bide;
And thus from life to death I slide,
As cold sometimes as any stone;
And then again as hot anon.

Thus come and go my sundry fits,
To give me sundry sorts of wits;
Till that a sigh becomes my friend,
And then too all this woe doth end.
And sure I think, that sigh doth run
From me to you, whereas you won.
For well I find it easeth me;
And certès much it pleaseth me,
To think that it doth come to you,
As, would to God, it could so do.
For then I know you would soon find,
By scent and savour of the wind,
That even a martyr's sigh it is,
Whose joy you are, and all his bliss;
His comfort and his pleasure eke,
And even the same that he doth seek;
The same that he doth wish and crave;
The same that he doth trust to have;
To tender you in all he may,
And all your likings to obey,

[1] Overpowered with sorrow.

As far as in his power shall lie;
Till death shall dart him, for to die.

   But well-away! mine own most best,
My joy, my comfort, and my rest;
The causer of my woe and smart,
And yet the pleaser of my heart;
And she that on the earth above
Is even the worthiest for to love,
Hear now my plaint! hear now my woe!
Hear now his pain that loves you so!
And if your heart do pity bear,
Pity the cause that you shall hear.

   A doleful foe in all this doubt,
Who leaves me not, but seeks me out,
Of wretched form and loathsome face,
While I stand in this woful case,
Comes forth, and takes me by the hand,
And says, ' Friend, hark! and understand;
I see well by thy port and chere,
And by thy looks and thy manere,
And by thy sadness as thou goest,
And by the sighs that thou out throwest,
That thou art stuffed full of woe.
The cause, I think, I do well know.
A fantaser thou art of some,
By whom thy wits are overcome.
But hast thou read old pamphlets aught?
Or hast thou known how books have taught
That love doth use to such as thou?
When they do think them safe enow,

And certain of their ladies' grace,
Hast thou not seen ofttimes the case,
That suddenly their hap hath turn'd?
As things in flame consum'd and burn'd.
Some by deceit forsaken right;
Some likewise changed of fancy light;
And some by absence soon forgot.
The lots in love, why knowest thou not?
And though that she be now thine own,
And knows thee well, as may be known;
And thinks thee to be such a one
As she likes best to be her own;
Think'st thou that others have not grace,
To shew and plain their woful case?
And choose her for their lady now;
And swear her truth as well as thou?
And what if she do alter mind,
Where is the love that thou wouldst find?
Absence, my friend, works wonders oft;
Now brings full low that lay full loft;
Now turns the mind, now to, now fro' [1]
And where art thou, if it were so?'
  'If absence,' quoth I, be marvellous,
I find her not so dangerous;
For she may not remove me fro'.
The poor good will that I do owe
To her, whom erst [2] I love, and shall;
And chosen have above them all,

1 In the early copies, "now to and low."
2 Long since; printed ed. uneath.

To serve and be her own as far
As any man may offer her;
And will her serve and will her love,
And lowly, as it shall behove;
And die her own, if fate be so:
Thus shall my heart nay part her fro'.
And witness shall my good will be,
That absence takes her not from me;
But that my love doth still increase
To mind her still, and never cease:
And what I feel to be in me,
The same good will, I think, hath she
As firm and fast to bidden aye,
Till death depart us both away.'
    And as I have my tale thus told,
Steps unto me, with countenance bold,
A steadfast friend, a counsellor,
And nam'd is, Hope, my comforter;
And stoutly then he speaks and says,
'Thou hast said truth withouten nays;
For I assure thee, even by oath,
And thereon take my hand and troth,
That she is one the worthiest,
The truest, and the faithfullest;
The gentlest and the meekest of mind,
That here on earth a man may find:
And if that love and truth were gone,
In her it might be found alone.
For in her mind no thought there is,
But how she may be true, I wis;

And tenders thee, and all thy heal,
And wisheth both thy health and weal;
And loves thee even as far-forth than
As any woman may a man;
And is thine own, and so she says;
And cares for thee ten thousand ways.
On thee she speaks, on thee she thinks;
With thee she eats, with thee she drinks;
With thee she talks, with thee she moans;
With thee she sighs, with thee she groans;
With thee she says, 'Farewell, mine own!'
When thou, God knows, full far art gone.
And even, to tell thee all aright,
To thee she says full oft, 'Good night!'
And names thee oft her own most dear,
Her comfort, weal, and all her cheer;
And tells her pillow all the tale
How thou hast done her woe and bale;
And how she longs, and plains for thee,
And says, 'Why art thou so from me?
Am I not she that loves thee best?
Do I not wish thine ease and rest?
Seek I not how I may thee please?
Why art thou then so from thine ease?
If I be she for whom thou carest,
For whom in torments so thou farest,
Alas! thou knowest to find me here,
Where I remain thine own most dear;
Thine own most true, thine own most just;
Thine own that loves thee still, and must;

Thine own that cares alone for thee,
As thou, I think, dost care [for] me;
And even the woman, she alone
That is full bent to be thine own.'
    'What wilt thou more? what canst thou crave?
Since she is as thou wouldst her have.
Then set this drivel out of door,
That in thy brains such tales doth pour,
Of absence, and of changes strange;
Send him to those that use to change:
For she is none I thee avow,
And well thou mayst believe me now.'
When Hope hath thus his reason said,
Lord! how I feel me well a-paid!
A new blood then o'erspreads my bones,
That all in joy I stand at ones.
My hands I throw to heav'n above,
And humbly thank the god of love;
That of his grace I should bestow
My love so well as I it owe.
And all the planets as they stand,
I thank them too with heart and hand;
That their aspects so friendly were,
That I should so my good will bear;
To you, that are the worthiest,
The fairest, and the gentleëst;
And best can say, and best can do
That 'longs, methinks, a woman to;
And therefore are most worthy far,
To be beloved as you are.

And so says Hope in all his tale,
Whereby he easeth all my bale.
For I believe, and think it true
That he doth speak or say of you.
And thus contented, lo! I stand
With that, that hope bears me in hand,
That you are mine, and shall so be.
Which hope I keep full sure in me,
As he, that all my comfort is.
On you alone, which are my bliss,
My pleasure chief, which most I find,
And e'en the whole joy of my mind.
And shall so be, until the death
Shall make me yield up life and breath.
Thus, good mine own, lo! here my trust
Lo! here my truth, and service just;
Lo! in what case for you I stand!
Lo! how you have me in your hand;
And if you can requite a man,
Requite me, as you find me than.

6

ECCLESIASTES.

CHAPTER I.

I, SOLOMON, David's son, King of Jerusalem,
Chosen by God to teach the Jews, and in his laws
    to lead them,
Confess, under the Sun that every thing is vain;
The world is false; man he is frail, and all his
    pleasures pain.
Alas! what stable fruit may Adam's children find
In that they seek by sweat of brows and travail of
    their mind!
We, that live on the earth, draw toward our decay;
Our children fill our place a while, and then they
    vade [1] away.
Such changes makes the earth, and doth remove
    for none;
But serves us for a place to play our tragedies upon.
When that the restless sun westward his course
    hath run,
Towards the east he hastes as fast to rise where
    he begun.
When hoary Boreas hath blown his frozen blast,
Then Zephyrus, with his gentle breath, dissolves the
    ice as fast.

[1] Go, or pass.

Floods that drink up small brooks, and swell by
    rage of rain,
Discharge in seas; which them repulse, and swallow
    straight again.
These worldly pleasures, Lord! so swift they run
    their race,
That scarce our eyes may them discern; they bide
    so little space.
What hath been but is now; the like hereafter
    shall:
What new device grounded so sure, that dreadeth
    not the fall!
What may be called new, but such things in times
    past
As Time buried, and doth revive; and Time again
    shall waste.
Things past right worthy fame, have now no bruit
    at all;
Even so shall die such things as now the simple
    wonders call.
I, that in David's seat sit crowned, and rejoice,
That with my sceptre rule the Jews, and teach them
    with my voice,
Have searched long to know all things under the
    sun;
To see how in this mortal life a surety might be won.
This kindled will to know; strange things for to
    desire,
God hath graft in our greedy breasts a torment
    for our hire.

The end of each travail forthwith I sought to know;
I found them vain, mixed with gall, and burthen'd
        with much woe.
Defaults of nature's work no man's hand may re-
        store,
Which be in number like the sands upon the salt
        floods shore.
Then vaunting in my wit, I gan call to my mind
What rules of wisdom I had taught, that elders
        could not find.
And, as by contraries to try most things we use,
Men's follies, and their errors eke I gan them all
        peruse;
Thereby with more delight to knowledge for to climb:
But this I found an endless work of pain, and loss
        of time.
For he to wisdom's school that doth apply his mind,
The further that he wades therein, the greater doubts
        shall find.
And such as enterprise to put new things in ure,
Of some that shall scorn their device, may well
        themselves assure.

CHAPTER II.

From pensive fancies then I gan my heart revoke;
And gave me to such sporting plays as laughter
        might provoke:
But even such vain delights, when they most blinded
        me,   [ill agree.
Always, methought, with smiling grace a king did

Then sought I how to please my belly with much
    wine,
To feed me fat with costly feasts of rare delights,
    and fine ;
And other pleasures eke to purchase me, with rest:
In so great choice to find the thing that might
    content me best.
But, Lord! what care of mind, what sudden storms
    of ire,
What broken sleeps endured I, to compass my
    desire.
To build me houses fair then set I all my cure :
By princely acts thus strove I still to make my
    fame endure.
Delicious gardens eke I made to please my sight;
And graft therein all kinds of fruits that might my
    mouth delight.
Conduits, by lively springs from their old course I
    drew,
For to refresh the fruitful trees that in my gardens
    grew.
Of cattle great increase I bred in little space;
Bondmen I bought; I gave them wives, and serv'd
    me with their race.
Great heaps of shining gold by sparing gan I save;
With things of price so furnished as fits a prince to
    have.
To hear fair women sing sometime I did rejoice;
Ravished with their pleasant tunes, and sweetness
    of their voice.

Lemans I had, so fair and of so lively hue,
That whoso gazed in their face might well their
    beauty rue.
Never erst sat there king so rich in David's seat;
Yet still, methought, for so small gain the travail
    was too great.
From my desirous eyes I hid no pleasant sight,
Nor from my heart no kind of mirth that might
    give them delight;
Which was the only fruit I reap'd of all my pain,
To feed my eyes, and to rejoice my heart, with all
    my gain.
But when I made my count, with how great care of
    mind
And hearts unrest, that I had sought so wasteful
    fruit to find;
Then was I striken straight with that abused fire,
To glory in that goodly wit that compass'd my
    desire.
But fresh before mine eyes grace did my faults
    renew:
What gentle callings I had fled my ruin to pursue;
What raging pleasures past, peril and hard escape;
What fancies in my head had wrought the liquor of
    the grape.
The error then I saw that their frail hearts doth
    move,
Which strive in vain for to compare with Him that
    sits above :

In whose most perfect works such craft appeareth
    plain,
That to the least of them, there may no mortal hand
    attain.
And like as lightsome day doth shine above the
    night,
So dark to me did folly seem, and wisdom's beams
    as bright,
Whose eyes did seem so clear motes to discern and
    find:
But Will had closed Folly's eyes, which groped like
    the blind.
Yet death and time consume all wit and worldly
    fame;
And look! what end that folly hath, and wisdom
    hath the same.
Then said I thus: 'Oh Lord! may not thy wisdom
    cure
The wailful wrongs and hard conflicts that folly doth
    endure?'
To sharp my wit so fine then why took I this pain?
Now find I well this noble search may eke be
    called vain.
As slander's loathsome bruit sounds folly's just
    reward,
Is put to silence all betime, and brought in small
    regard:
Even so doth time devour the noble blast of fame,
Which should resound their glories great that do
    deserve the same.

Thus present changes chase away the wonders past,
Ne is the wise man's fatal thread yet longer spun
     to last.
Then in this wretched vale, our life I loathed plain,
When I beheld our fruitless pains to compass pleas-
     ures vain.
My travail this avail hath me produced, lo!
An heir unknown shall reap the fruit that I in seed
     did sow.
But whereunto the Lord his nature shall incline
Who can foreknow, into whose hands I must my
     goods resign.
But, Lord, how pleasant sweet then seem'd the idle
     life,
That never charged was with care, nor burthened
     with strife.
And vile the greedy trade of them that toil so sore,
To leave to such their travails fruit that never sweat
     therefore.
What is that pleasant gain? what is that sweet re-
     lief,
That should delay the bitter taste that we feel of our
     grief?
The gladsome days we pass to search a simple gain;
The quiet nights, with broken sleeps, to feed a rest-
     less brain.
What hope is left us then? What comfort doth
     remain?
Our quiet hearts for to rejoice with the fruit of our
     pain.

If that be true, who may himself so happy call
As I whose free and sumptuous spence doth shine
      beyond them all?
Surely it is a gift and favour of the Lord,
Liberally to spend our goods, the ground of all
      discord.
And wretched hearts have they that let their treas-
      ures mould,
And carry the rod that scourgeth them that glory in
      their gold.
But I do know, by proof, whose riches bear such
      bruit,
What stable wealth may stand in waste, or heaping
      of such fruit.

CHAPTER III.

Like to the steerless boat that swerves with every
      wind,
The slipper top of worldly wealth, by cruel proof
      I find.   [man,
Scarce hath the seed, whereof that nature formeth
Received life, when death him yields to earth where
      he began!   [fruit,
The grafted plants with pain, whereof we hoped
To root them up, with blossoms spread, then is our
      chief pursuit.
That erst we reared up, we undermine again;
And shred the sprays whose growth sometime we
      laboured with pain.

Each froward threat'ning chere of fortune makes us
    plain;

And every pleasant show revives our woful hearts
    again.

Ancient walls to rase is our unstable guise;

And of their weather-beaten stones, to build some
    new device.

New fancies daily spring, which vade,[1] returning
    mo';

And now we practise to obtain that straight we must
    forego.

Some time we seek to spare that afterward we
    waste;

And that we travail'd sore to knit, for to unloose as
    fast.

In sober silence now our quiet lips we close;

And with unbridled tongues forthwith our secret
    hearts disclose.

Such as in folded arms we did embrace, we hate;

Whom straight we reconcile again, and banish all
    debate.

My seed with labour sown, such fruit produceth
    me,

To waste my life in contraries that never shall agree.

From God these heavy cares are sent for our un-
    rests;

And with such burdens for our wealth he fraughteth
    full our breasts.

---

1 Pass away.

All that the Lord hath wrought, hath beauty and
    good grace;
And to each thing assigned is the proper time and
    place.
And granted eke to man of all the world's estate,
And of each thing wrought in the same, to argue
    and debate.
Which art, though it approach the heavenly know-
    ledge most,
To search the natural ground of things, — yet all is
    labour lost.
But then the wandering eyes that long for surety
    sought,
Found that by pain no certain wealth might in this
    world be bought.
Who liveth in delight and seeks no greedy thrift,
But freely spends his goods, may think it is a se-
    cret gift.
Fulfilled shall it be what so the Lord intend;
Which no device of man's wit may advance, nor
    yet defend;
Who made all things of nought, that Adam's chil-
    dren might
Learn how to dread the Lord, that wrought such
    wonders in their sight.
The grisly wonders past, which time wears out of
    mind,
To be renewed in our days the Lord hath so as-
    sign'd.   [ware;
Lo! thus his careful scourge doth steal on us un-

Which, when the flesh hath clean forgot, he doth
    again repair.
When I in this vain search had wander'd sore my
    wit,
I saw a royal throne eke where as Justice should
    have sit.
Instead of whom I saw, with fierce and cruel mood,
Where wrong was set; that bloody beast that drank
    the guiltless blood:
Then thought I thus: ' One day the Lord shall sit
    in doom,
To view his flock, and choose the pure; the spotted
    have no room.'
Yet be such scourges sent, that each aggrieved mind
Like the brute beasts that swell in rage and fury by
    their kind,
His error may confess when he hath wrestled long;
And then with patience may him arm: the sure
    defence of wrong.
For death, that of the beast the carrion doth de-
    vour,
Unto the noble kind of man presents the fatal hour.
The perfect form that God hath given to either man,
Or other beast, dissolve it shall to earth, where it
    began.
And who can tell if that the soul of man ascend;
Or with the body if it die, and to the ground de-
    scend.
Wherefore each greedy heart that riches seeks to
    gain,

Gather may he that savoury fruit that springeth of
    his pain.
A mean convenient wealth I mean to take in worth;
And with a hand of largess eke in measure pour it
    forth.
For treasure spent in life the body doth sustain;
The heir shall waste the hoarded gold, amassed with
    much pain.
Nor may foresight of man such order give in life,
For to foreknow who shall enjoy their gotten good
    with strife.

CHAPTER IV.

When I bethought me well, under the restless Sun
By folk of power what cruel works unchastised
    were done;
I saw where stood a herd by power of such opprest,
Out of whose eyes ran floods of tears, that bayned [1]
    all their breast;
Devoid of comfort clean, in terrors and distress;
In whose defence none would arise such rigour to
    repress.
Then thought I thus: 'Oh Lord! the dead whose
    fatal hour
Is clean run out more happy are; whom that the
    worms devour:
And happiest is the seed that never did conceive;

---

[1] Bathed.

That never felt the wailful wrongs that mortal folk
    receive.'
And then I saw that wealth, and every honest gain
By travail won, and sweat of brows, gan grow into
    disdain,
Through sloth of careless folk, whom ease so fat
    doth feed;
Whose idle hands do nought but waste the fruit of
    other's seed.
Which to themselves persuade — that little got with
    ease
More thankful is, than kingdoms won by travail and
    disease.
Another sort I saw without both friend or kin,
Whose greedy ways yet never sought a faithful friend
    to win.
Whose wretched corpse no toil yet ever weary
    could;
Nor glutted ever were their eyes with heaps of
    shining gold.
But, if it might appear to their abused eyen,
To whose avail they travail so, and for whose sake
    they pine;
Then should they see what cause they have for to
    repent
The fruitless pains and eke the time that they in
    vain have spent.
Then gan I thus resolve — 'More pleasant is the life
Of faithful friends that spend their goods in common,
    without strife.'

For as the tender friend appeaseth every grief,
So, if he fall that lives alone, who shall be his re-
    lief?
The friendly feeres[1] lie warm in arms embraced
    fast;
Who sleeps alone, at every turn doth feel the win-
    ter blast:
What can he do but yield, that must resist alone?
If there be twain, one may defend the t'other over-
    thrown.
The single twined cords may no such stress endure
As cables braided threefold may, together wreathed
    sure.
In better far estate stand children, poor and wise,
Than aged kings, wedded to will, that work without
    advice.
In prison have I seen, or this, a woful wight
That never knew what freedom meant, nor tasted
    of delight;
With such unhoped hap in most despair hath met,
Within the hands that erst wore gyves to have a
    sceptre set.
And by conjures[2] the seed of kings is thrust from
    state,
Whereon a grieved people work ofttimes their hid-
    den hate.
Other, without respect, I saw a friend or foe
With feet worn bare in tracing such, whereas the
    honours grew.

[1] Companions.   [2] Conspiracies.

And at death of a prince great routs revived strange,
Which fain their old yoke to discharge, rejoiced in
     the change.
But when I thought, to these as heavy even or more
Shall be the burden of his reign, as his that went
     before;
And that a train like great upon the dead attend,
I gan conclude, each greedy gain hath its uncertain
     end.
In humble spirit is set the temple of the Lord;
Where if thou enter, look thy mouth and conscience
     may accord!
Whose Church is built of love, and deckt with hot
     desire,
And simple faith; the yolden ghost his mercy doth
     require.
Where perfectly for aye he in his word doth rest;
With gentle ear to hear thy suit, and grant thee thy
     request.
In boast of outward works he taketh no delight,
Nor waste of words; such sacrifice unsavoureth in
     his sight.

CHAPTER V.

When that repentant tears hath cleansed clear
     from ill
The charged breast; and grace hath wrought there-
     in amending will;

With bold demands then may his mercy well assail
The speech man saith, without the which request
    may none prevail.
More shall thy penitent sighs his endless mercy
    please,
Than their importune suits, which dream that words
    God's wrath appease.
For heart, contrite of fault, is gladsome recom-
    pense;
And prayer, fruit of Faith, whereby God doth with
    sin dispense.
As fearful broken sleeps spring from a restless head,
By chattering of unholy lips is fruitless prayer bred.
In waste of wind, I rede,[1] vow nought unto the Lord,
Whereto thy heart to bind thy will, freely doth not
    accord;
For humble vows fulfill'd, by grace right sweetly
    smoke:
But bold behests, broken by lusts, the wrath of God
    provoke.
Yet bet[2] with humble heart thy frailty to confess,
Than to boast of such perfectness, whose works such
    fraud express.
With feigned words and oaths contract with God no
    guile;
Such craft returns to thine own harm, and doth thy-
    self defile.
And though the mist of sin persuade such error
    light,

---

[1] I advise.   [2] Better.

Thereby yet are thy outward works all dampned in
    his sight.
As sundry broken dreams us diversly abuse,
So are his errors manifold that many words doth
    use.
With humble secret plaint, few words of hot effect,
Honour thy Lord; allowance vain of void desert
    neglect.
Though wrong at times the right, and wealth eke
    need oppress,
Think not the hand of justice slow to follow the
    redress.
For such unrighteous folk as rule withouten dread,
By some abuse or secret lust he suffereth to be led. .
The chief bliss that in earth to living man is lent,
Is moderate wealth to nourish life, if he can be
    content.
He that hath but one field, and greedily seeketh
    nought,
To fence the tiller's hand from need, is king within
    his thought.
But such as of their gold their only idol make,
No treasure may the raven of their hungry hands
    aslake.
For he that gapes for good, and hoardeth all his
    gain,
Travails in vain to hide the sweet that should relieve
    his pain.
Where is great wealth, there should be many a
    needy wight

To spend the same; and that should be the rich
    man's chief delight.
The sweet and quiet sleeps that wearied limbs op-
    press,
Beguile the night in diet thin, not feasts of great
    excess:
But waker [1] lie the rich; whose lively heat with rest
Their charged bulks [2] with change of meats cannot
    so soon digest.
Another righteous doom I saw of greedy gain;
With busy cares such treasures oft preserved to
    their bane:
The plenteous houses sackt, the owners end with
    shame
Their sparkled goods; their needy heirs, that should
    enjoy the same,
From wealth despoiled bare, from whence they came
    they went;
Clad in the clothes of poverty, as Nature first them
    sent.
Naked as from the womb we came, if we depart,
With toil to seek that we must leave, what boot
    to vex the heart?
What life lead testy men then, that consume their
    days
In inward frets, untemper'd hates, at strife with
    some always.
Then gan I praise all those, in such a world of
    strife,

[1] Wakeful.   [2] Bodies.

As take the profit of their goods, that may be had
    in life.
For sure the liberal hand that hath no heart to
    spare
This fading wealth, but pours it forth, it is a virtue
    rare :
That makes wealth slave to need, and gold become
    his thrall,
Clings [1] not his guts with niggish [2] fare, to heap his
    chest withal;
But feeds the lusts of kind with costly meats and
    wine;
And slacks the hunger and the thirst of needy folk
    that pine.
No glutton's feast I mean in waste of spence [3] to
    strive;
But temperate meals the dulled spirits with joy thus
    to revive.
No care may pierce where mirth hath temper'd such
    a breast:
The bitter gall, season'd with sweet, such wisdom
    may digest.

[1] Starve.   [2] Niggard.   [3] Expense.

A PARAPHRASE OF SOME OF THE PSALMS
OF DAVID.

PROEM.

WHERE rechless[1] youth in an unquiet breast,
Set on by wrath, revenge, and cruelty,
After long war patience had oppress'd;
And justice, wrought by princely equity;
My DENNY[2] then, mine error deep imprest,
Began to work despair of liberty;
Had not David, the perfect warrior taught,
That of my fault thus pardon should be sought.

PSALM LXXXVIII.

O Lord! upon whose will dependeth my welfare,
To call upon thy holy name, since day nor night I
    spare,
Grant that the just request of this repentant mind
So pierce thine ears, that in thy sight some favour
    it may find.
My soul is fraughted full with grief of follies past;

[1] Careless.
[2] In the old edition the name does not occur, and the word ' conscience' is substituted. Dr. Nott suggests that this person was " Sir Walter Denny, an intimate friend of the Howard family, and afterwards one of the executors of Henry the Eighth's will."

My restless body doth consume, and death ap-
    proacheth fast:

Like them whose fatal thread, thy hand hath cut in
    twain;

Of whom there is no further bruit, which in their
    graves remain.

Oh Lord! thou hast me cast headlong, to please
    my foe,

Into a pit all bottomless, whereas I plain my woe.

The burden of thy wrath it doth me sore oppress;

And sundry storms thou hast me sent of terror and
    distress.

The faithful friends are fled and banished from my
    sight:

And such as I have held full dear, have set my
    friendship light.

My durance doth persuade of freedom such de-
    spair,

That by the tears that bain my breast, mine eye-
    sight doth appair.[1]

Yet do I never cease thine aid for to desire,

With humble heart and stretched hands, for to ap-
    pease thine ire.

Wherefore dost thou forbear in the defence of thine,

To shew such tokens of thy power in sight of Adam's
    line;   [fed,

Whereby each feeble heart with faith might so be

That in the mouth of thy elect thy mercies might be
    spread.

[1] Fail.

The flesh that feedeth worms cannot thy love de-
 clare!
Nor such set forth thy praise as dwell in the land
 of despair.
In blind indured hearts light of thy lively name
Cannot appear, nor cannot judge the brightness of
 the same.
Nor blazed may thy name be by the mouths of those
Whom death hath shut in silence, so as they may
 not disclose.
The lively voice of them that in thy word delight,
Must be the trump that must resound the glory of
 thy might.
Wherefore I shall not cease, in chief of my distress
To call on Thee, till that the sleep my wearied limbs
 oppress.
And in the morning eke when that the sleep is fled,
With floods of salt repentant tears to wash my rest-
 less bed.
Within this careful mind, burden'd with care and
 grief,
Why dost thou not appear, Oh Lord! that shouldst
 be his relief.
My wretched state behold, whom death shall straight
 assail;
Of one, from youth afflicted still, that never did but
 wail.
The dread, lo! of thine ire hath trod me under feet:
The scourges of thine angry hand hath made death
 seem full sweet.

Like as the roaring waves the sunken ship surround,
Great heaps of care did swallow me, and I no suc-
      cour found :
For they whom no mischance could from my love
      divide,
Are forced, for my greater grief, from me their face
      to hide.

PSALM LXXIII.

The sudden storms that heave me to and fro,
Had well near pierced Faith, my guiding sail;
For I that on the noble voyage go
To succour truth, and falsehood to assail,
Constrained am to bear my sails full low;
And never could attain some pleasant gale.
For unto such the prosperous winds do blow
As run from port to port to seek avail.[1]
This bred despair; whereof such doubts did grow
That I gan faint, and all my courage fail.
But now, my BLAGE,[2] mine error well I see;
Such goodly light king David giveth me.

[1] Advantage.
[2] "Blame" in the old edition. George Blage, a friend of
Surrey's, who accompanied him to Landrecy. He was of a good
Kentish family, was educated at Cambridge, and addressed a
poem to Lord Wriothesley.

Though, Lord, to Israel thy graces plenteous be;

I mean to such, with pure intent as fix their trust in
       Thee,

Yet whiles the Faith did faint that should have
       been my guide,

Like them that walk in slipper paths, my feet began
       to slide;

Whiles I did grudge at those that glory in their
       gold,

Whose loathsome pride enjoyeth wealth, in quiet as
       they would.

To see by course of years what nature doth appair,[1]

The palaces of princely form succeed from heir to
       heir.

From all such travails free, as 'long to Adam's
       seed,

Neither withdrawn from wicked works by danger, nor
       by dread.

Whereof their scornful pride, and gloried with their
       eyes;

As garments clothe the naked man, thus are they
       clad in vice.

Thus, as they wish, succeeds the mischief that they
       mean;

Whose glutted cheeks sloth feeds so fat, as scant
       their eyes be seen.[2]

[1] Become weak; decay.
[2] This seems aimed at K. Henry VIII.

Unto whose cruel power most men for dread are
    fain
To bend or bow; with lofty looks, whiles they vaunt
    in their reign;
And in their bloody hands, whose cruelty that frame
The wailful works that scourge the poor, without
    regard of blame.
To tempt the living God they think it no offence;
And pierce the simple with· their tongues that can
    make no defence.
Such proofs before the just, to cause the hearts to
    waver,
Be set like cups mingled with gall, of bitter taste
    and savour.
Then say thy foes in scorn, that taste no other food,
But suck the flesh of thy Elect, and bathe them in
    their blood;
' Should we believe the Lord doth know, and suf-
    fer this?
Fooled be he with fables vain that so abused is.'
In terror of the just, that reigns iniquity,
Armed with power, laden with gold, and dread for
    cruelty.
Then vain the ·war might seem, that I by faith
    maintain
Against the flesh, whose false effects my pure heart
    would disdain.
For I am scourged still, that no offence have done,
By wrathès children; and from my birth my chas-
    tising begun.

When I beheld their pride, and slackness of thy
    hand,
I gan bewail the woful state wherein thy chosen
    stand.
And when I sought whereof thy sufferance, Lord,
    should grow,
I found no wit could pierce so far, thy holy dooms
    to know:
And that no mysteries, nor doubt could be distrust,
Till I come to the holy place, the mansion of the
    just;
Where I shall see what end thy justice shall pre-
    pare,
For such as build on worldly wealth, and dye their
    colours fair.
Oh! how their ground is false! and all their build-
    ing vain!
And they shall fall; their power shall fail that did
    their pride maintain.
As charged hearts with care, that dream some pleas-
    ant turn,
After their sleep find their abuse, and to their plaint
    return;   [shall
So shall their glory fade; thy sword of vengeance
Unto their drunken eyes in blood disclose their
    errors all.
And when their golden fleece is from their back
    y-shorn;
The spots that underneath were hid, thy chosen
    sheep shall scorn:

And till that happy day, my heart shall swell in
 care,
My eyes yield tears, my years consume between
 hope and despair.
Lo! how my spirits are dull, and all thy judgments
 dark,
No mortal head may scale so high, but wonder at
 thy work.
Alas! how oft my foes have framed my decay;
But when I stood in dread to drench,[1] thy hands
 still did me stay.
And in each voyage that I took to conquer sin,
Thou wert my guide, and gave me grace, to com-
 fort me therein.
And when my wither'd skin unto my bones did
 cleave,
And flesh did waste, thy grace did then my simple
 spirits relieve.
In other succour then, O Lord! why should I
 trust;
But only thine, whom I have found in thy behight[2]
 so just.
And such for dread, or gain as shall thy name re-
 fuse,
Shall perish with her golden gods that did their
 hearts seduce.
While[3] I, that in thy word have set my trust and
 joy,

[1] To be overwhelmed.   [2] Promise.   [3] MS. Where.

The high reward that 'longs thereto shall quietly
    enjoy.
And my unworthy lips, inspired with thy grace,
Shall thus forespeak thy secret works, in sight of
    Adam's race.

PSALM LV.

Give ear to my suit, Lord! fromward hide not thy
    face:
Behold! hearken, in grief, lamenting how I pray:
My foes that bray so loud, and eke threpe on[1] so
    fast,
Buckled to do me scath,[2] so is their malice bent.
Care pierceth my entrails, and travaileth my spirit;
The grisly fear of death environeth my breast:
A trembling cold of dread overwhelmeth my heart.
'O!' think I, 'had I wings like to the simple dove,
This peril might I fly; and seek some place of rest
In wilder woods, where I might dwell far from these
    cares.'
What speedy way of wing my plaints should they
    lay on,
To 'scape the stormy blast that threaten'd is to me?
Rein those unbridled tongues! break that conjured
    league!
For I decipher'd have amid our town the strife.
Guile and wrong keep the walls; they ward both
    day and night:

---

[1] To accuse with clamour.   [2] Injury.

And mischief join'd with care doth keep the market-
    stead :

Whilst wickedness with crafts in heaps swarm
    through the street.

Ne my declared foe wrought me all this reproach.

By harm so looked for, it weigheth half the less.

For though mine enemies hap had been for to pre-
    vail,

I could have hid my face from venom of his eye.

It was a friendly foe, by shadow of good will;

Mine old fere,[1] and dear friend, my guide that
    trapped me ;

Where I was wont to fetch the cure of all my care,

And in his bosom hide my secret zeal to God.

With such sudden surprise, quick may him hell de-
    vour ;

Whilst I invoke the Lord, whose power shall me
    defend,

My prayer shall not cease, from that the sun de-
    scends,

Till he his alture [2] win, and hide them in the sea.

With words of hot effect,[3] that moveth from heart
    contrite,   [ear.

Such humble suit, O Lord, doth pierce thy patient

It was the Lord that brake the bloody compacts of
    those

That pricked on with ire, to slaughter me and mine.

The everlasting God, whose kingdom hath no end,

---

[1] Companion.   [2] Altitude.   [3] Affection; passion.

Whom by no tale to dread he could divert from sin,
The conscience unquiet he strikes with heavy hand,
And proves their force in faith, whom he sware to
    defend.
Butter falls not so soft as doth his patience long,
And overpasseth fine oil running not half so smooth.
But when his sufferance finds that bridled wrath
    provokes,
His threatened wrath he whets more sharp than
    tool can file.
Friar! whose harm and tongue presents the wicked
    sort,
Of those false wolves, with coats which do their
    ravin hide;
That swear to me by heaven, the footstool of the
    Lord,
Though force had hurt my fame, they did not touch
    my life.
Such patching care I loath, as feeds the wealth with
    lies;
But in the other Psalm of David find I ease.
Jacta curam tuam super Dominum, et ipse te enu-
    triet.

PSALM VIII.

Thy name, O Lord, how great, is found before our
    sight!
It fills the earth, and spreads the air: the great
    works of thy might!

For even unto the heavens thy power hath given a
     place,
And closed it above their heads; a mighty, large,
     compass.
Thy praise what cloud can hide, but it will shine
     again:
Since young and tender sucking babes have power
     to shew it plain.
Which in despight of those that would thy glory
     hide,
[Thou] hast put into such infants' mouths for to
     confound their pride.
Wherefore I shall behold thy figur'd heaven so
     high,
Which shews such prints of divers forms within the
     cloudy sky:
As hills, and shapes of men; eke beasts of sundry
     kind,
Monstrous to our outward sight, and fancies of our
     mind.
And eke the wanish moon, which sheens by night
     also;
And each one of the wandering stars, which after
     her do go.
And how these keep their course; and which are
     those that stands;
Because they be thy wondrous works, and labours
     of thy hands.
But yet among all these I ask, 'What thing is
     man?'

Whose turn to serve in his poor need this work
    Thou first began.
Or what is Adam's son that bears his father's mark?
For whose delight and comfort eke Thou hast
    wrought all this work.
I see thou mind'st him much, that dost reward
    him so :
Being but earth, to rule the earth, whereon himself
    doth go.
From angel's substance eke Thou mad'st him differ
    small ;
Save one doth change his life awhile ; the other not
    at all.
The sun and moon also Thou mad'st to give him
    light ;
And each one of the wandering stars to twinkle
    sparkles bright.
The air to give him breath ; the water for his health ;
The earth to bring forth grain and fruit, for to in-
    crease his wealth.
And many metals too, for pleasure of the eye ;
Which in the hollow sounded ground in privy veins
    do lie.
The sheep to give his wool, to wrap his body in ;
And for such other needful things, the ox to spare
    his skin.
The horse even at his will to bear him to and fro :
And as him list each other beast to serve his turn
    also.
The fishes of the sea likewise to feed him oft ;

And eke the birds, whose feathers serve to make
    his sides lie soft.
On whose head thou hast set a crown of glory too,
To whom also thou didst appoint, that honour should
    be do.
And thus thou mad'st him lord of all this work of
    thine;
Of man that goes, of beast that creeps, whose looks
    doth down decline;
Of fish that swim below, of fowls that fly on high,
Of sea that finds the air his rain, and of the land
    so dry.
And underneath his feet, Thou hast set all this same;
To make him know, and plain confess, that mar-
    vellous is thy name.
And, Lord, which art our Lord, how marvellous it
    is found
The heavens do shew, the earth doth tell, and eke
    the world so round.
Glory, therefore, be given to Thee first, which art
    three;   [degree:
And yet but one Almighty God, in substance and
As first it was when Thou the dark confused heap,
Clotted in one, didst part in four; which elements
    we clepe:[1]
And as the same is now, even here within our time;
So[2] ever shall hereafter be, when we be filth and
    slime.

---

[1] We call.   [2] MS. And.

THE SECOND BOOK OF VIRGIL'S ÆNEID.

THEY whisted all, with fixed face attent,
When prince Æneas from the royal seat
Thus gan to speak.   O Queen! it is thy will
I should renew a woe cannot be told:
How that the Greeks did spoil, and overthrow
The Phrygian wealth, and wailful realm of Troy:
Those ruthful things that I myself beheld;
And whereof no small part fell to my share.
Which to express, who could refrain from tears?
What Myrmidon? or yet what Dolopes?
What stern Ulysses' waged soldier?
And lo! moist night now from the welkin falls;
And stars declining counsel us to rest.
But since so great is thy delight to hear
Of our mishaps, and Troyè's last decay;
Though to record the same my mind abhors,
And plaint eschews, yet thus will I begin.
    The Greeks' chieftains all irked with the war
Wherein they wasted had so many years,
And oft repuls'd by fatal destiny,
A huge horse made, high raised like a hill,
By the divine science of Minerva:
Of cloven fir compacted were his ribs;
For their return a feigned sacrifice .

The fame whereof so wander'd it at point.
In the dark bulk they clos'd bodies of men
Chosen by lot, and did enstuff by stealth
The hollow womb with armed soldiers.

   There stands in sight an isle, hight Tenedon,
Rich, and of fame, while Priam's kingdom stood;
Now but a bay, and road, unsure for ship.
Hither them secretly the Greeks withdrew,
Shrouding themselves under the desert shore.
And, weening we they had been fled and gone,
And with that wind had fet the land of Greece,
Troy discharged her long continued dole.
The gates cast up, we issued out to play,
The Greekish camp desirous to behold,
The places void, and the forsaken coasts.
' Here Pyrrhus' band; there fierce Achilles pight;
Here rode their ships; there did their battles join.'
Astonnied some the scatheful gift beheld,
Behight by vow unto the chaste Minerve;
All wond'ring at the hugeness of the horse.

   And first of all Timœtes gan advise
Within the walls to lead and draw the same;
And place it eke amid the palace court:
Whether of guile, or Troyè's fate it would.
Capys, with some of judgment more discreet,
Will'd it to drown; or underset with flame
The suspect present of the Greeks' deceit;
Or bore and gage the hollow caves uncouth.
So diverse ran the giddy people's mind.

Lo! foremost of a rout that follow'd him,
Kindled Laocoon hasted from the tower,
Crying far off: 'O wretched citizens!
What so great kind of frenzy fretteth you?
Deem ye the Greeks our enemies to be gone?
Or any Greekish gifts can you suppose
Devoid of guile?   Is so Ulysses known?
Either the Greeks are in this timber hid;
Or this an engine is to annoy our walls,
To view our towers, and overwhelm our town.
Here lurks some craft. Good Troyans! give no trust
Unto this horse; for what so ever it be,
I dread the Greeks; yea! when they offer gifts.'
And with that word, with all his force a dart
He lanced then into that crooked womb;
Which trembling stuck, and shook within the side:
Wherewith the caves gan hollowly resound.
And, but for Fates, and for our blind forecast,
The Greeks' device and guile had he descried;
Troy yet had stood, and Priam's towers so high.
    Therewith behold, whereas the Phrygian herds
Brought to the king with clamour, all unknown
A young man, bound his hands behind his back;
Who willingly had yielden prisoner,
To frame this guile, and open Troyè's gates
Unto the Greeks; with courage fully bent,
And mind determed either of the twain;
To work his feat, or willing yield to death.
Near him, to gaze, the Trojan youth gan flock,

And strove who most might at the captive scorn.
The Greeks' deceit behold, and by one proof
Imagine all the rest.

    For in the press as he unarmed stood
With troubled cheer, and Phrygian routs beset;
' Alas!' quod he, ' what earth now, or what seas
May me receive? catiff, what rests me now?
For whom in Greece doth no abode remain.
The Trojans eke offended seek to wreak
Their heinous wrath, with shedding of my blood.'

    With this regret our hearts from rancour moved.
The bruit appeas'd, we ask'd him of his birth,
What news he brought; what hope made him to
       yield.

    Then he, all dread removed, thus began:
' O King! I shall what ever me betide,
Say but the truth: ne first will me deny
A Grecian born; for though fortune hath made
Sinon a wretch, she cannot make him false.
If ever came unto your ears the name,
Nobled by fame, of the sage Palamede,
Whom trait'rously the Greeks condemn'd to die;
Guiltless, by wrongful doom, for that he did
Dissuade the wars; whose death they now lament;
Underneath him my father, bare of wealth,
Into his band young, and near of his blood,
In my prime years unto the war me sent.
While that by fate his state in stay did stand,
And when his realm did flourish by advice,

Of glory, then, we bare some fame and bruit.
But since his death by false Ulysses' sleight,
(I speak of things to all men well beknown)
A dreary life in doleful plaint I led,
Repining at my guiltless friend's mischance.
Ne could I, fool! refrain my tongue from threats,
That if my chance were ever to return
Victor to Arge, to follow my revenge.
With such sharp words procured I great hate.
Here sprang my harm.   Ulysses ever sith
With new found crimes began me to affray.
In common ears false rumours gan he sow:
Weapons of wreak his guilty mind gan seek.
Ne rested aye till he by Calchas mean ————
But whereunto these thankless tales in vain
Do I rehearse, and linger forth the time,
In like estate if all the Greeks ye price?
It is enough ye here rid me at once.
Ulysses, Lord! how he would this rejoice!
Yea, and either Atride would buy it dear.'
    This kindled us more eager to inquire,
And to demand the cause; without suspect
Of so great mischief thereby to ensue,
Or of Greeks' craft.   He then with forged words
And quivering limbs, thus took his tale again.
    'The Greeks oftimes intended their return
From Troyè town, with long wars all ytired,
And to dislodge; which, would God! they had done.
But oft the winter storms of raging seas,

And oft the boisterous winds did them to stay;
And chiefly, when of clinched ribs of fir
This horse was made, the storms roared in the air.
Then we in doubt to Phœbus' temple sent
Euripilus, to weet the prophesy.
From whence he brought these woful news again.
With blood, O Greeks! and slaughter of a maid,
Ye peas'd the winds, when first ye came to Troy.
With blood likewise ye must seek your return:
A Greekish soul must offer'd be therefore.'
   'But when this sound had pierc'd the peoples'
      ears,
With sudden fear astonied were their minds;
The chilling cold did overrun their bones,
To whom that fate was shap'd, whom Phœbus
      would.'
Ulysses then amid the press brings in
Calchas with noise, and will'd him to discuss
The Gods' intent. Then some gan deem to me
The cruel wreak of him that fram'd the craft;
Foreseeing secretly what would ensue.
In silence then, yshrowding him from sight,
But days twice five he whisted; and refused
To death, by speech, to further any wight.
At last, as forced by false Ulysses' cry,
Of purpose he brake forth, assigning me
To the altar; whereto they granted all:
And that, that erst each one dread to himself,
Returned all unto my wretched death.

And now at hand drew near the woful day.
All things prepar'd wherewith to offer me;
Salt, corn, fillets, my temples for to bind.
I scap'd the death, I grant! and brake the bands,
And lurked in a marish all the night
Among the ooze, while they did set their sails;
If it so be that they indeed so did.
Now rests no hope my native land to see,
My children dear, nor long desired sire;
On whom, perchance, they shall wreak my escape:
Those harmless wights shall for my fault be slain.
  'Then, by the gods, to whom all truth is known;
By faith unfil'd, if any anywhere
With mortal folk remains; I thee beseech,
O king, thereby rue on my travail great:
Pity a wretch that guiltless suffereth wrong.'
  Life to these tears with pardon eke, we grant.
And Priam first himself commands to loose
His gyves, his bands; and friendly to him said:
'Whoso thou art, learn to forget the Greeks:
Henceforth be ours; and answer me with truth:
Whereto was wrought the mass of this huge horse?
Whose the devise? and whereto should it tend?
What holy vow? or engine for the wars?'
  Then he, instruct with wiles and Greekish craft,
His loosed hands lift upward to the stars:
'Ye everlasting lamps! I testify,
Whose power divine may not be violate;
Th' altar, and sword,' quoth he, 'that I have scap'd;

Ye sacred bands! I wore as yielden host;
Lawful be it for me to break mine oath
To Greeks; lawful to hate their nation;
Lawful be it to sparkle in the air
Their secrets all, whatso they keep in close:
For free am I from Greece and from their laws.
So be it, Troy, and saved by me from scathe,
Keep faith with me, and stand to thy behest;
If I speak truth, and opening things of weight,
For grant of life requite thee large amends.
  'The Greeks' whole hope of undertaken war
In Pallas' help consisted evermore.
But sith the time that wicked Diomed,
Ulysses eke, that forger of all guile,
Adventur'd from the holy sacred fane
For to bereave Dame Pallas' fatal form,
And slew the watches of the chiefest tower.
And then away the holy statue stole;
(That were so bold with hands embrued in blood,
The virgin Goddess veils for to defile)
Sith then their hope gan fail, their hope to fall,
Their pow'r appair, their Goddess' grace withdraw
Which with no doubtful signs she did declare.
Scarce was the statue to our tents ybrought,
But she gan stare with sparkled eyes of flame;
Along her limbs the salt sweat trickled down:
Yea thrice herself, a hideous thing to tell!
In glances bright she glittered from the ground,
Holding in hand her targe and quivering spear.

Calchas by sea then bade us haste our flight:
Whose engines might not break the walls of Troy,
Unless at Greece they would renew their lots,
Restore the God that they by sea had brought
In warped keels.   To Arge sith they be come,
They 'pease their Gods, and war afresh prepare.
And cross the seas unlooked for eftsoons
They will return.   This order Calchas set.
　' This figure made they for th' aggrieved God,
In Pallas' stead; to cleanse their heinous fault.
Which mass he willed to be reared high
Toward the skies, and ribbed all with oak,
So that your gates ne wall might it receive;
Ne yet your people might defensed be
By the good zeal of old devotion.
For if your hands did Pallas' gift defile,
To Priam's realm great mischief should befall:
Which fate the Gods first on himself return.
But had your own hands brought it in your town,
Asia should pass, and carry offer'd war
In Greece, e'en to the walls of Pelop's town;
And we and ours that destiny endure.'
　By such like wiles of Sinon, the forsworn,
His tale with us did purchase credit; some,
Trapt by deceit; some, forced by his tears;
Whom neither Diomed, nor great Achille,
.Nor ten years war, ne a thousand sail could daunt.
　Us caitiffs then a far more dreadful chance
Befel, that troubled our unarmed breasts.

Whiles Laocoon, that chosen was by lot
Neptunus' priest, did sacrifice a bull
Before the holy altar; suddenly
From Tenedon, behold! in circles great
By the calm seas come fleeting adders twain,
Which plied towards the shore (I loathe to tell)
With reared breast lift up above the seas:
Whose bloody crests aloft the waves were seen;
The hinder part swam hidden in the flood.
Their grisly backs were linked manifold.
With sound of broken waves they gat the strand,
With glowing eyen, tainted with blood and fire;
Whose waltring tongues did lick their hissing mouths.
We fled away; our face the blood forsook:
But they with gait direct to Lacon ran.
And first of all each serpent doth enwrap
The bodies small of his two tender sons;
Whose wretched limbs they bit, and fed thereon.
Then raught they him, who had his weapon caught
To rescue them; twice winding him about,
With folded knots and circled tails, his waist:
Their scaled backs did compass twice his neck,
With reared heads aloft and stretched throats.
He with his hands strave to unloose the knots,
(Whose sacred fillets all-besprinkled were
With filth of gory blood, and venom rank)
And to the stars such dreadful shouts he sent,
Like to the sound the roaring bull forth lows,
Which from the altar wounded doth astart,

The swerving axe when he shakes from his neck.
The serpents twain, with hasted trail they glide
To Pallas' temple, and her towers of height:
Under the feet of the which Goddess stern,
Hidden behind her target's boss they crept.
New gripes of dread then pierce our trembling
      breasts.
They said; Lacon's deserts had dearly bought
His heinous deed; that pierced had with steel
The sacred bulk, and thrown the wicked lance.
The people cried with sundry greeing shouts
To bring the horse to Pallas' temple blive;
In hope thereby the Goddess' wrath t' appease.
We cleft the walls and closures of the town;
Whereto all help: and underset the feet
With sliding rolls, and bound his neck with ropes.
This fatal gin thus overclamb our walls,
Stuft with arm'd men; about the which there ran
Children and maids, that holy carols sang;
And well were they whose hands might touch the
      cords.
With threat'ning cheer thus slided through our
      town
The subtle tree, to Pallas' temple-ward.
O native land! Ilion! and of the Gods
The mansion place!   O warlike walls of Troy!
Four times it stopt in th' entry of our gate;
Four times the harness clatter'd in the womb.
But we go on, unsound of memory,

And blinded eke by rage persever still:
This fatal monster in the fane we place.

   Cassandra then, inspired with Phœbus sprite,
Her prophet's lips, yet never of us 'lieved,
Disclosed eft; forespeaking things to come.
We wretches, lo! that last day of our life
With boughs of feast the town, and temples deck.

   With this the sky gan whirl about the sphere:
The cloudy night gan thicken from the sea,
With mantles spread; that cloaked earth and
     skies,
And eke the treason of the Greekish guile.
The watchmen lay dispers'd to take their rest;
Whose wearied limbs sound sleep had then op-
     press'd:
When, well in order comes the Grecian fleet
From Tenedon, toward the coasts well known,
By friendly silence of the quiet moon.
When the king's ship put forth his mark of fire,
Sinon, preserved by froward destiny,
Let forth the Greeks enclosed in the womb:
The closures eke of pine by stealth unpinn'd,
Whereby the Greeks restored were to air.
With joy down hasting from the hollow tree,
With cords let down did slide unto the ground
The great captains; Sthenel, and Thessander,
And fierce Ulysses, Athamas, and Thoas;
Machaon first, and then king Menelae;
Opeas eke that did the engine forge.

And straight invade the town yburied then
With wine and sleep.   And first the watch is slain:
Then gates unfold to let their fellows in,
They join themselves with the conjured bands.
   It was the time when granted from the Gods
The first sleep creeps most sweet in weary folk.
Lo! in my dream before mine eyes, methought,
With rueful cheer I saw where Hector stood,
(Out of whose eyes there gushed streams of tears)
Drawn at a car as he of late had be,
Distained with bloody dust, whose feet were bowln
With the strait cords wherewith they hailed him.
Ay me, what one? that Hector how unlike,
Which erst return'd clad with Achilles' spoils;
Or when he threw into the Greekish ships
The Trojan flame! so was his beard defiled,
His crisped locks all clust'red with his blood,
With all such wounds, as many he received
About the walls of that his native town.
Whom frankly thus methought I spake unto,
With bitter tears and doleful deadly voice:
'O Troyan light! O only hope of thine!
What lets so long thee staid? or from what coasts,
Our most desired Hector, dost thou come?
Whom, after slaughter of thy many friends,
And travail of the people, and thy town,
All-wearied lord! how gladly we behold.
What sorry chance hath stain'd thy lively face?
Or why see I these wounds, alas! so wide?'

He answer'd nought, nor in my vain demands
Abode; but from the bottom of his breast
Sighing he said: ' Flee, flee, O Goddess' son!
And save thee from the fury of this flame.
Our en'mies now are masters of the walls; .
And Troyè town now falleth from the top.
Sufficeth that is done for Priam's reign.
If force might serve to succour Troyè town,
This right hand well might have been her defence.
But Troyè now commendeth to thy charge
Her holy reliques, and her privy Gods.
Them join to thee, as fellows of thy fate.
Large walls rear thou for them: for so thou shalt,
After time spent in th' overwand'red flood.'
This said, he brought forth Vesta in his hands;
Her fillets eke, and everlasting flame.
· In this mean while with diverse plaint, the town
Throughout was spread; and louder more and more
The din resounded: with rattling of arms,
Although mine old Father Anchises' house
Removed stood, with shadow hid of trees,
I waked: therewith to the house-top I clamb,
And hark'ning stood I: like as when the flame
Lights in the corn, by drift of boisterous wind;
Or the swift stream that driveth from the hill,
Roots up the fields, and presseth the ripe corn,
And ploughed ground, and overwhelms the grove:
The silly herdman all astonnied stands,
From the high rock while he doth hear the sound.

Then the Greeks' faith, then their deceit ap-
    peared.
Of Deiphobus the palace large and great
Fell to the ground, all overspread with flash.
His next neighbour Ucalegon afire:
The Sygean seas did glister all with flame.
Up sprang the cry of men, and trumpets blast.
Then, as distraught, I did my armour on;
Ne could I tell yet whereto arms avail'd.
But with our feres to throng out from the press
Toward the tower, our hearts brent with desire.
Wrath prick'd us forth; and unto us it seemed
A seemly thing to die, arm'd in the field.
    Wherewith Panthus scap'd from the Greekish
    darts,
Otreus' son, Phœbus' priest, brought in hand
The sacred reliques, and the vanquish'd Gods:
And in his hand his little nephew led;
And thus, as phren'tic, to our gates he ran.
'Panthus,' quod I, 'in what estate stand we?
Or for refuge what fortress shall we take?'
Scarce spake I this, when wailing thus he said:
'The latter day, and fate of Troy is come;
The which no plaint, or prayer may avail.
Troyans we were; and Troyè was sometime,
And of great fame the Teucrian glory erst:
Fierce Jove to Grecce hath now transposed all.
The Greeks are lords over this fired town.
Yonder huge horse that stands amid our walls
    9

Sheds armed men: and Sinon, victor now,
With scorn of us doth set all things on flame.
And, rushed in at our unfolded gates,
Are thousands mo' than ever came from Greece.
And some with weapons watch the narrow streets;
With bright swords drawn, to slaughter ready bent.
And scarce the watches of the gate began
Them to defend, and with blind fight resist.'
　　Through Panthus' words, and lightning of the
　　　　Gods,
Amid the flame and arms ran I in press,
As fury guided me, and whereas I had heard
The cry greatest that made the air resound.
Into our band then fell old Iphytus,
And Rypheus, that met us by moonlight;
Dymas and Hypanis joining to our side,
With young Chorebus, Mygdonius' son;
Which in those days at Troy did arrive,
(Burning with rage of dame Cassandra's love)
In Priam's aid, and rescue of his town.
Unhappy he! that would no credit give
Unto his spouse's words of prophecy.
　　Whom when I saw, assembled in such wise,
So desperately the battle to desire;
Then furthermore thus said I unto them:
'O! ye young men, of courage stout in vain!
For nought ye strive to save the burning town.
What cruel fortune hath betid, ye see!
The Gods out of the temples all are fled,

Through whose might long this empire was main-
    tain'd:
Their altars eke are left both waste and void.
But if your will be bent with me to prove
That uttermost, that now may us befall;
Then let us die, and run amid our foes.
To vanquish'd folk, despair is only hope.'

  With this the young men's courage did increase;
And through the dark, like to the ravening wolves
Whom raging fury of their empty maws
Drives from their den, leaving with hungry throat
Their whelps behind; among our foes we ran,
Upon their swords, unto apparent death;
Holding alway the chief street of the town,
Cover'd with the close shadows of the night.

  Who can express the slaughter of that night?
Or tell the number of the corpses slain?
Or can in tears bewail them worthily?
The ancient famous city falleth down,
That many years did hold such seignory.
With senseless bodies every street is spread,
Each palace, and sacred porch of the gods.
Nor yet alone the Troyan blood was shed.
Manhood ofttimes into the vanquish'd breast
Returns, whereby some victors Greeks are slain.
Cruel complaints, and terror everywhere,
And plenty of grisly pictures of death.

  And first with us Androgeus there met,
Fellowed with a swarming rout of Greeks,

Deeming us, unware, of that fellowship,
With friendly words whom thus he call'd unto:
' Haste ye, my friends ! what sloth hath tarried you ?
Your feres now sack and spoil the burning Troy:
From the tall ships were ye but newly come ? '
　　When he had said, and heard no answer made
To him again, whereto he might give trust;
Finding himself chanced amid his foes,
'Maz'd he withdrew his foot back with his word:
Like him that wand'ring in the bushes thick,
Treads on the adder with his reckless foot,
Reared for wrath, swelling her speckled neck,
Dismay'd, gives back all suddenly for fear:
Androgeus so, fear'd of that sight, stept back,
And we gan rush amid the thickest rout;
When, here and there we did them overthrow,
Stricken with dread, unskilful of the place.
Our first labour thus lucked well with us.
　　Chorebus then, encouraged by this chance,
Rejoicing said: ' Hold forth the way of health,
My feres, that hap and manhood hath us taught.
Change we our shields; the Greeks' arms do we on.
Craft or manhood with foes what recks it which:
The slain to us their armour they shall yield.'
And with that word Androgeus' crested helm
And the rich arms of his shield did he on;
A Greekish sword he girded by his side:
Like gladly Dimas and Ripheus did:
The whole youth gan them clad in the new spoils.

Mingled with Greeks, for no good luck to us,
We went, and gave many onsets that night,
And many a Greek we sent to Pluto's court.
Other there fled and hasted to their ships,
And to their coasts of safeguard ran again.
And some there were for shameful cowardry,
Clamb up again unto the hugy horse,
And did them hide in his well knowen womb.
  Ay me! bootless it is for any wight
To hope on aught against will of the gods.
Lo! where Cassandra, Priam's daughter dear,
From Pallas' church was drawn with sparkled tress,
Lifting in vain her flaming eyen to heaven;
Her eyen, for fast her tender wrists were bound.
Which sight Chorebus raging could not bear,
Reckless of death, but thrust amid the throng;
And after we through thickest of the swords.
  Here were we first y-batter'd with the darts
Of our own feres, from the high temples' top;
Whereby of us great slaughter did ensue,
Mistaken by our Greekish arms and crests.
Then flock'd the Greeks moved with wrath and ire,
Of the virgin from them so rescued.
The fell Ajax; and either Atrides,
And the great band cleped the Dolopes.
As wrestling winds, out of dispersed whirl
Befight themselves, the west with southern blast,
And gladsome east proud of Aurora's horse;
The woods do whiz; and foamy Nereus

Raging in fury, with three forked mace
From bottom's depth doth welter up the seas;
So came the Greeks.   And such, as by deceit
We sparkled erst in shadow of the night,
And drave about our town, appeared first:
Our feigned shields and weapons then they found,
And, by sound, our discording voice they knew.
We went to wreck with number overlaid.
And by the hand of Peneleus first
Chorebus fell before the altar dead
Of armed Pallas; and Rhipheus eke,
The justest man among the Troians all,
And he that best observed equity.
But otherwise it pleased now the Gods.
There Hypanis, and Dymas, both were slain;
Through pierced with the weapons of their feres.
Nor thee, Panthus, when thou wast overthrown,
Pity, nor zeal of good devotion,
Nor habit yet of Phœbus hid from scath.

  Ye Troyan ashes! and last flames of mine!
I call in witness, that at your last fall
I fled no stroke of any Greekish sword.
And if the fates would I had fallen in fight,
That with my hand I did deserve it well.

  With this from thence I was recoiled back
With Iphytus and Pelias alone.
Iphytus weak, and feeble all for age;
Pelias lamed by Ulysses' hand.
To Priam's palace cry did call us then.

Here was the fight right hideous to behold;
As though there had no battle been but there,
Or slaughter made elsewhere throughout the town.
A fight of rage and fury there we saw.
The Greeks toward the palace rushed fast,
And cover'd with engines the gates beset,
And reared up ladders against the walls;
Under the windows scaling by their steps,
Fenced with shields in their left hands, whereon
They did receive the darts; while their right hands
Griped for hold th' embattle of the wall.
The Troyans on the other part rend down
The turrets high, and eke the palace roof;
With such weapons they shope them to defend,
Seeing all lost, now at the point of death.
The gilt spars, and the beams then threw they down;
Of old fathers the proud and royal works.
And with drawn swords some did beset the gates,
Which they did watch, and keep in routs full thick.
Our sprites restor'd to rescue the king's house,
To help them, and to give the vanquish'd strength.

   A postern with a blind wicket there was,
A common trade to pass through Priam's house;
On the back side whereof waste houses stood:
Which way eft-sithes, while that our kingdom
       dured,
Th' infortunate Andromache alone
Resorted to the parents of her make;
With young Astyanax, his grandsire to see.

Here passed I up to the highest tower,
From whence the wretched Troyans did throw **down**
Darts, spent in waste.   Unto a turret then
We stept, the which stood in a place aloft,
The top whereof did reach well near the stars;
Where we were wont all Troyè to behold,
The Greekish navy, and their tents also.
With instruments of iron gan we pick,
To seek where we might find the joining shrunk
From that high seat; which we razed, and **threw**
      down:
Which falling, gave forthwith a rushing sound,
And large in breadth on Greekish routs it light.
But soon another sort stept in their stead;
No stone unthrown, nor yet no dart uncast.
   Before the gate stood Pyrrhus in the porch
Rejoicing in his darts, with glittering arms.
Like to th' adder with venemous herbès fed,
Whom cold winter all bolne, hid under ground;
And shining bright, when she her slough had **slung**,
Her slipper back doth roll, with forked tongue
And raised breast, lift up against the sun.
With that together came great Periphas;
Automedon eke, that guided had some time
Achilles' horse, now Pyrrhus armour bare;
And eke with him the warlike Scyrian youth
Assail'd the house; and threw flame to the top.
And he an axe before the foremost raught,
Wherewith he gan the strong gates hew, and **break**;

From whence he beat the staples out of brass,
He brake the bars, and through the timber pierc'd
So large a hole, whereby they might discern
The house, the court, the secret chambers eke
Of Priamus, and ancient kings of Troy;
And armed foes in th' entry of the gate.

   But the palace within confounded was,
With wailing, and with rueful shrieks and cries;
The hollow halls did howl of women's plaint:
The clamour strake up to the golden stars.
The 'fray'd mothers, wand'ring through the wide
      house,
Embracing pillars, did them hold and kiss.
Pyrrhus assaileth with his father's might;
Whom the closures ne keepers might hold out.
With often pushed ram the gate did shake;
The posts beat down, removed from their hooks:
By force they made the way, and th' entry brake.
And now the Greeks let in, the foremost slew:
And the large palace with soldiers gan to fill.
Not so fiercely doth overflow the fields
The foaming flood, that breaks out of his banks;
Whose rage of waters bears away what heaps
Stand in his way, the cotes, and eke the herds.
As in th' entry of slaughter furious
I saw Pyrrhus, and either Atrides.

   There Hecuba I saw, with a hundred mo'
Of her sons' wives, and Priam at the altar,
Sprinkling with blood his flame of sacrifice.

Fifty bed-chambers of his children's wives,
With loss of so great hope of his offspring,
The pillars eke proudly beset with gold,
And with the spoils of other nations,
Fell to the ground: and what so that with flame
Untouched was, the Greeks did all possess.

    Percase you would ask what was Priam's fate?
When of his taken town he saw the chance,
And the gates of his palace beaten down,
His foes amid his secret chambers eke:
Th' old man in vain did on his shoulders then,
Trembling for age, his cuirass long disused:
His bootless sword he girded him about;
And ran amid his foes, ready to die.

    Amid the court, under the heaven, all bare,
A great altar there stood, by which there grew
An old laurel tree, bowing thereunto,
Which with his shadow did embrace the gods.
Here Hecuba, with her young daughters all
About the altar swarmed were in vain;
Like doves, that flock together in the storm,
The statues of the Gods embracing fast.
But when she saw Priam had taken there
His armour, like as though he had been young:
'What furious thought my wretched spouse,' **quod**
      she,
'Did move thee now such weapons for to wield?
Why hastest thou?   This time doth not require
Such succour, ne yet such defenders now:

No, though Hector my son were here again.
Come hither; this altar shall save us all:
Or we shall die together.'   Thus she said.
Wherewith she drew him back to her, and set
The aged man down in the holy seat.

But lo! Polites, one of Priam's sons,
Escaped from the slaughter of Pyrrhus,
Comes fleeing through the weapons of his foes,
Searching, all wounded, the long galleries
And the void courts; whom Pyrrhus all in rage
Followed fast to reach a mortal wound;
And now in hand, well near strikes with his spear.
Who fleeing forth till he came now in sight
Of his parents, before their face fell down
Yielding the ghost with flowing streams of blood.
Priamus then, although he were half dead,
Might not keep in his wrath, nor yet his words;
But crieth out: 'For this thy wicked work,
And boldness eke such thing to enterprise,
If in the heavens any justice be,
That of such things takes any care or keep,
According thanks the Gods may yield to thee;
And send thee eke thy just deserved hire,
That made me see the slaughter of my child,
And with his blood defile the father's face.
But he, by whom thou feign'st thyself begot,
Achilles, was to Priam not so stern.
For, lo! he tend'ring my most humble suit,
The right, and faith, my Hector's bloodless corpse

Render'd, for to be laid in sepulture;
And sent me to my kingdom home again.'
    Thus said the aged man, and therewithal,
Forceless he cast his weak unwieldy dart.
Which repuls'd from the brass where it gave dint,
Without sound, hung vainly in the shield's boss.
Quod Pyrrhus: 'Then thou shalt this thing re-
        port:
On message to Pelide my father go:
Shew unto him my cruel deeds, and how
Neoptolem is swerved out of kind.
Now shalt thou die,' quod he.   And with that word
At the altar him trembling 'gan he draw
Wallowing through the bloodshed of his son:
And his left hand all clapsed in his hair,
With his right arm drew forth his shining sword,
Which in his side he thrust up to the hilts.
Of Priamus this was the fatal fine,
The woful end that was allotted him,
When he had seen his palace all on flame,
With ruin of his Troyan turrets eke.
That royal prince of Asia, which of late
Reign'd over so many peoples and realms,
Like a great stock now lieth on the shore;
His head and shoulders parted been in twain:
A body now without renown and fame.
    Then first in me enter'd the grisly fear:
Dismay'd I was.   Wherewith came to my mind
The image eke of my dear father, when

I thus beheld the king of equal age,
Yield up the spirit with wounds so cruelly.
Then thought I of Creusa left alone;
And of my house in danger of the spoil,
And the estate of young Iulus eke.
I looked back to seek what number then
I might discern about me of my feres:
But wearied they had left me all alone.
Some to the ground were lopen from above,
Some in the flame their irked bodies cast.

There was no mo' but I left of them all,
When that I saw in Vesta's temple sit,
Dame Helen, lurking in a secret place;
Such light the flame did give as I went by
While here and there I cast mine eyen about:
For she in dread lest that the Troians should
Revenge on her the ruin of their walls;
And of the Greeks the cruel wreaks also;
The fury eke of her forsaken make,
The common bane of Troy, and eke of Greece!
Hateful she sat beside the altars hid.
Then boil'd my breast with flame, and burning
          wrath,
To revenge my town, unto such ruin brought;
With worthy pains on her to work my will.
Thought I: " Shall she pass to the land of Sparte
All safe, and see Mycene her native land,
And like a queen return with victory
Home to her spouse, her parents, and children,

Followed with a train of Troyan maids,
And served with a band of Phrygian slaves;
And Priam eke with iron murder'd thus,
And Troyè town consumed all with flame,
Whose shore hath been so oft for-bathed in blood?
No! no! for though on women the revenge
Unseemly is; such conquest hath no fame:
To give an end unto such mischief yet
My just revenge shall merit worthy praise;
And quiet eke my mind, for to be wroke
On her which was the causer of this flame,
And satisfy the cinder of my feres.'

   With furious mind while I did argue thus,
My blessed mother then appear'd to me,
Whom erst so bright mine eyes had never seen,
And with pure light she glistred in the night,
Disclosing her in form a goddess like,
As she doth seem to such as dwell in heaven.
My right hand then she took, and held it fast,
And with her rosy lips thus did she say:
'Son! what fury hath thus provoked thee
To such untamed wrath? what ragest thou?
Or where is now become the care of us?
Wilt thou not first go see where thou hast left
Anchises, thy father fordone with age?
Doth Creusa live, and Ascanius thy son?
Whom now the Greekish bands have round beset:
And were they not defenced by my cure,
Flame had them raught, and en'mies' sword ere this.

Not Helen's beauty hateful unto thee,
Nor blamed Paris yet, but the Gods' wrath
Reft you this wealth, and overthrew your town.
Behold ! and I shall now the cloud remove,
Which overcast thy mortal sight doth dim ;
Whose moisture doth obscure all things about:
And fear not thou to do thy mother's will,
Nor her advice refuse thou to perform.
Here, where thou see'st the turrets overthrown,
Stone beat from stone, smoke rising mixt with dust,
Neptunus there shakes with his mace the walls,
And eke the loose foundations of the same,
And overwhelms the whole town from his seat:
And cruel Juno with the foremost here
Doth keep the gate that Scea cleped is,
Near woode for wrath, whereas she stands, and calls
In harness bright the Greeks out of their ships:
And in the turrets high behold where stands
Bright shining Pallas, all in warlike weed,
And with her shield, where Gorgon's head appears:
And Jupiter, my father, distributes
Availing strength, and courage to the Greeks;
Yet overmore, against the Troyan power
He doth provoke the rest of all the Gods.
Flee then, my son, and give this travail end;
Ne shall I thee forsake, in safeguard till
I have thee brought unto thy father's gate.'
This did she say : and therewith gan she hide
Herself, in shadow of the close night.

Then dreadful figures gan appear to me,
And great Gods eke aggrieved with our town.
I saw Troyè fall down in burning gledes;
Neptunus town, clean razed from the soil.
Like as the elm forgrown in mountains high,
Round hewen with axe, that husbandmen
With thick assaults strive to tear up, doth threat;
And hack'd beneath trembling doth bend his top,
Till yold with strokes, giving the latter crack,
Rent from the height, with ruin it doth fall.
  With this I went, and guided by a God
I passed through my foes, and eke the flame:
Their weapons and the fire eke gave me place.
And when that I was come before the gates,
And ancient building of my father's house;
My father, whom I hoped to convey
To the next hills, and did him thereto 'treat,
Refused either to prolong his life,
Or bide exile after the fall of Troy.
'All ye,' quod he, 'in whom young blood is fresh,
Whose strength remains entire and in full power,
Take ye your flight.
For if the Gods my life would have prorogued,
They had reserved for me this wonning place.
It was enough, alas! and eke too much,
To see the town of Troy thus razed once;
To have lived after the city taken.
When ye have said, this corpse laid out forsake;
My hand shall seek my death, and pity shall

Mine en'mies move, or else hope of my spoil.
As for my grave, I weigh the loss but light:
For I my years, disdainful to the Gods,
Have lingered forth, unable to all needs,
Since that the Sire of Gods and king of men
Strake me with thunder, and with levening blast.'
Such things he gan rehearse, thus firmly bent:
But we besprent with tears, my tender son,
And eke my sweet Creusa, with the rest
Of the household, my father 'gan beseech,
Not so with him to perish all at once,
Nor so to yield unto the cruel fate:
Which he refused, and stack to his intent.

 Driven I was to harness then again,
Miserably my death for to desire.
For what advice, or other hope was left?
'Father! thought'st thou that I may once remove,'
Quod I, 'a foot, and leave thee here behind?
May such a wrong pass from a father's mouth?
If God's will be, that nothing here be saved
Of this great town, and thy mind bent to join
Both thee and thine to ruin of this town:
The way is plain this death for to attain.
Pyrrhus shall come besprent with Priam's blood,
That gor'd the son before the father's face,
And slew the father at the altar eke.
O sacred Mother! was it then for this
That you me led through flame, and weapons
  sharp,

That I might in my secret chamber see
Mine en'mies; and Ascanius my son,
My father, with Creusa my sweet wife,
Murder'd, alas! the one in th' others' blood?
Why, servants! then, bring me my arms again.
The latter day us vanquished doth call.
Render me now to the Greeks' sight again:
And let me see the fight begun of new:
We shall not all unwroken die this day.'
  About me then I girt my sword again,
And eke my shield on my left shoulder cast,
And bent me so to rush out of the house.
Lo! in my gate my spouse, clasping my feet,
For against his father young Iulus set.
'If thou wilt go,' quod she, 'and spill thyself,
Take us with thee in all that may betide.
But as expert if thou in arms have set
Yet any hope, then first this house defend,
Whereas thy son, and eke thy father dear,
And I, sometime thine own dear wife, are left.'
Her shrill loud voice with plaint thus fill'd the
       house;
When that a sudden monstrous marvel fell:
For in their sight, and woful parents' arms,
Behold a light out of the butten sprang
That in tip of Iulus cap did stand;
With gentle touch whose harmless flame did shine
Upon his hair, about his temples spread.
And we afraid, trembling for dreadful fear,

Bet out the fire from his blazing tress,
And with water 'gan quench the sacred flame.
   Anchises glad his eyen lift to the stars ;
With hands his voice to heaven thus he bent.
'If by prayer, almighty Jupiter,
Inclined thou mayst be, behold us then
Of ruth at least, if we so much deserve.
Grant eke thine aid, Father! confirm this thing.'
   Scarce had the old man said, when that the
      heavens
With sudden noise thunder'd on the left hand :
Out of the sky, by the dark night there fell
A blazing star, dragging a brand or flame,
Which with much light gliding on the house top,
In the forest of Ida hid her beams ;
The which full bright cendleing a furrow, shone,
By a long tract appointing us the way :
And round about of brimstone rose a fume.
   My father vanquish'd then, beheld the skies,
Spake to the Gods, and th' holy star adored :
'Now, now,' quod he, 'no longer I abide :
Follow I shall where ye me guide at hand.
O native Gods! your family defend ;
Preserve your line, this warning comes of you,
And Troyè stands in your protection now.
Now give I place, and whereso that thou go,
Refuse I not, my son, to be thy fere.'
   This did he say ; and by that time more clear
The cracking flame was heard throughout the walls,

And more and more the burning heat drew near.
'Why then! have done, my father dear,' quod I,
'Bestride my neck forthwith, and sit thereon,
And I shall with my shoulders thee sustain,
Ne shall this labour do me any dere.
What so betide, come peril, come welfare,
Like to us both and common there shall be.
Young Iulus shall bear me company;
And my wife shall follow far off my steps.
Now ye, my servants, mark well what I say:
Without the town ye shall find, on a hill,
An old temple there stands, whereas some time
Worship was done to Ceres the Goddess;
Beside which grows an aged cypress tree,
Preserved long by our forfathers' zeal:
Behind which place let us together meet.
And thou, Father, receive into thy hands
The reliques all, and the Gods of the land:
The which it were not lawful I should touch,
That come but late from slaughter and bloodshed,
Till I be washed in the running flood.'
   When I had said these words, my shoulders
      broad,
And laied neck with garments 'gan I spread,
And thereon cast a yellow lion's skin;
And thereupon my burden I receive.
Young Iulus clasped in my right hand,
Followeth me fast with unegal pace;
And at my back my wife.   Thus did we pass

By places shadowed most with the night.
And me, whom late the dart which enemies threw,
Nor press of Argive routs could make amaz'd,
Each whisp'ring wind hath power now to fray,
And every sound to move my doubtful mind:
So much I dread my burden, and my fere.

    And now we 'gan draw near unto the gate,
Right well escap'd the danger, as me thought,
When that at hand a sound of feet we heard.
My father then, gazing throughout the dark,
Cried on me, ' Flee, son! they are at hand.'
With that bright shields, and shene armours I saw.
But then, I know not what unfriendly God
My troubled wit from me bereft for fear:
For while I ran by the most secret streets,
Eschewing still the common haunted track,
From me catif, alas! bereaved was
Creusa then, my spouse, I wot not how;
Whether by fate, or missing of the way,
Or that she was by weariness retain'd:
But never sith these eyes might her behold;
Nor did I yet perceive that she was lost,
Ne never backward turned I my mind,
Till we came to the hill, whereas there stood
The old temple dedicate to Ceres.

    And when that we were there assembled all,
She was only away, deceiving us
Her spouse, her son, and all her company.
What God or man did I not then accuse,

Near woode for ire? or what more cruel chance
Did hap to me, in all Troy's overthrow?
Ascanius to my feres I then betook,
With Anchises, and eke the Troyan Gods.
And left them hid within a valley deep.
And to the town I 'gan me hie again,
Clad in bright arms, and bent for to renew
Aventures past, to search throughout the town,
And yield my head to perils once again.
  And first the walls and dark entry I sought
Of the same gate whereat I issued out;
Holding backward the steps where we had come
In the dark night, looking all round about:
In every place the ugsome sights I saw;
The silence self of night aghast my sprite.
From hence again I pass'd unto our house,
If she by chance had been returned home.
The Greeks were there, and had it all beset:
The wasting fire, blown up by drift of wind,
Above the roofs the blazing flame sprang up;
The sound whereof with fury pierc'd the skies.
To Priam's palace, and the castle then
I made; and there at Juno's sanctuair,
In the void porches, Phenix, Ulysses eke
Stern guardians stood, watching of the spoil.
The riches here were set, reft from the brent
Temples of Troy: the tables of the Gods,
The vessels eke that were of massy gold,
And vestures spoil'd, were gather'd all in heap:

The children orderly, and mothers pale for fright,
Long ranged on a row stood round about.
  So bold was I to show my voice that night
With clepes and cries to fill the streets throughout,
With Creuse' name in sorrow, with vain tears;
And often sithes the same for to repeat.
The town restless with fury as I sought,
Th' unlucky figure of Creusa's ghost,
Of stature more than wont, stood 'fore mine eyen.
Abashed when I woxe: therewith my hair
'Gan start right up: my voice stack in my throat:
When with such words she 'gan my heart remove:
' What helps, to yield unto such furious rage,
Sweet spouse?' quod she, ' Without will of the
        Gods
This chanced not: ne lawful was for thee
To lead away Creusa hence with thee:
The King of the high heaven suff'reth it not.
A long exile thou art assigned to bear,
Long to furrow large space of stormy seas:
So shalt thou reach at last Hesperian land,
Where Lidian Tiber with his gentle stream
Mildly doth flow along the fruitful fields.
There mirthful wealth, there kingdom is for thee;
There a king's child prepar'd to be thy make.
For thy beloved Creusa stint thy tears:
For now shall I not see the proud abodes
Of Myrmidons, nor yet of Dolopes:
Ne I, a Troyan lady, and the wife

Unto the son of Venus, the Goddess,
Shall go a slave to serve the Greekish dames.
Me here the God's great mother holds ———
And now farewell: and keep in father's breast
The tender love of thy young son and mine.'
    This having said, she left me all in tears,
And minding much to speak; but she was gone,
And subtly fled into the weightless air.
Thrice raught I with mine arms t' accoll her neck:
Thrice did my hands vain hold th' image escape,
Like nimble winds, and like the flying dream.
So night spent out, return I to my feres;
And there wond'ring I find together swarm'd
A new number of mates, mothers, and men
A rout exiled, a wretched multitude,
From each-where flock together, prest to pass
With heart and goods, to whatsoever land
By sliding seas, me listed them to lead.
And now rose Lucifer above the ridge
Of lusty Ide, and brought the dawning light.
The Greeks held th' entries of the gates beset:
Of help there was no hope.   Then gave I place,
Took up my sire, and hasted to the hill.

THE FOURTH BOOK OF VIRGIL'S ÆNEID.

But now the wounded Queen, with heavy care,
Throughout the veins she nourished the plaie,
Surprised with blind flame; and to her mind
'Gan eke resort the prowess of the man,
And honour of his race: while in her breast
Imprinted stack his words, and pictures form.
Ne to her limbs care granteth quiet rest.
　The next morrow, with Phœbus' lamp the earth
Alighted clear; and eke the dawning day
The shadows dark 'gan from the pole remove:
When all unsound, her sister of like mind
Thus spake she to: 'O! Sister Anne, what dreams
Be these, that me tormented thus affray?
What new guest this, that to our realm is come?
What one of cheer? how stout of heart in arms?
Truly I think (ne vain is my belief)
Of Goddish race some offspring should he be:
Cowardry notes hearts swerved out of kind.
He driven, lord! with how hard destiny!
What battles eke achieved did he recount!
But that my mind is fixt unmovably,
Never with wight in wedlock aye to join,
Sith my first love me left by death dissever'd;
If genial brands and bed me loathed not,
To this one guilt perchance yet might I yield.

Anne, for I grant, sith wretched Sichee's death,
My spouse and house with brother's slaughter
      stain'd,
This only man hath made my senses bend,
And pricked forth the mind that 'gan to slide:
Now feelingly I taste the steps of mine old flame.
But first I wish the earth me swallow down,
Or with thunder the mighty Lord me send
To the pale ghosts of hell, and darkness deep;
Ere I thee stain, shamefastness, or thy laws.
He that with me first coupled, took away
My love with him; enjoy it in his grave.'
   Thus did she say, and with surprised tears
Bained her breast. Whereto Anne thus replied:
  'O Sister, dearer beloved than the light:
Thy youth alone in plaint still wilt thou spill?
Ne children sweet, ne Venus' gifts wilt know?
Cinders, thinkest thou, mind this? or graved
      ghosts?
Time of thy doole, thy spouse new dead, I grant,
None might thee move: no, not the Libyan king,
Nor yet of Tyre; Iarbas set to light,
And other princes mo'; whom the rich soil
Of Afric breeds, in honours triumphant.
Wilt thou also gainstand thy liked love?
Comes not to mind upon whose land thou dwell'st?
On this side, lo! the Getule town behold,
A people bold, unvanquished in war;
Eke the undaunted Numides compass thee;

Also the Sirtes unfriendly harbrough.
On th' other hand, a desert realm for-thrust,
The Barceans, whose fury stretcheth wide.
What shall I touch the wars that move from Tyre?
Or yet thy brother's threats? ——
By Gods' purveyance it blew, and Juno's help,
The Troiaynes ships, I think, to run this course.
Sister, what town shalt thou see this become?
Through such ally how shall our kingdom rise?
And by the aid of Troyan arms how great?
How many ways shall Carthages glory grow?
Thou only now beseech the Gods of grace
By sacrifice: which ended, to thy house
Receive him, and forge causes of abode:
Whiles winter frets the seas, and wat'ry Orion,
The ships shaken, unfriendly the season.'
   Such words inflamed the kindled mind with love,
Loosed all shame, and gave the doubtful hope.
And to the temples first they haste, and seek
By sacrifice for grace, with hogrels of two years,
Chosen, as ought, to Ceres that gave laws,
To Phœbus, Bacchus, and to Juno chief,
Which hath in care the bands of marriage.
Fair Dido held in her right hand the cup,
Which 'twixt the horns of a white cow she shed
In presence of the Gods, passing before
The altars fat; which she renewed oft
With gifts that day, and beasts deboweled;
Gazing for counsel on the entrails warm.

Ay me! unskilful minds of prophesy!
Temples or vows, what boot they in her rage?
A gentle flame the marrow doth devour,
Whiles in the breast the silent wound keeps life.
Unhappy Dido burns, and in her rage
Throughout the town she wand'reth up and down.
Like the stricken hind with shaft, in Crete
Throughout the woods which chasing with his dart
Aloof, the shepherd smiteth at unwares,
And leaves unwist in her the thirling head:
That through the groves, and lands glides in her
        flight;
Amid whose side the mortal arrow sticks.
    Æneas now about the walls she leads,
The town prepared, and Carthage wealth to shew,
Off'ring to speak, amid her voice, she whists.
And when the day gan fail new feasts she makes;
The Troies travails to hear a-new she lists,
Enraged all; and stareth in his face
That tells the tale.   And when they were all gone,
And the dim moon doth eft withhold the light,
And sliding stars provoke unto sleep;
Alone she mourns within her palace void,
And sets her down on her forsaken bed.
And, absent, him she hears, when he is gone,
And seeth eke. Oft in her lap she holds
Ascanius, trapp'd by his father's form:
So to beguile the love, cannot be told.
    The turrets now arise not, erst begun;

Neither the youth wields arms, nor they advance
The ports, nor other meet defence for war:
Broken there hang the works and mighty frames
Of walls high raised, threatening the sky.
Whom as soon as Jove's dear wife saw infect
With such a plague, ne fame resist the rage;
Saturnès' daughter thus burdes Venus then:
' Great praise,' quod she, ' and worthy spoils you
        win,
You and your son; great Gods of memory!
By both your wiles one woman to devour.
Yet am not I deceived, that foreknew
Ye dread our walls, and buildings gan suspect
Of high Carthage.   But what shall be the end?
Or whereunto now serveth such debate?
But rather peace, and bridal bands knit we,
Sith thou hast sped of that thy heart desired;
Dido doth burn with love: rage frets her bones,
This people now as common to us both,
With equal favour let us govern then;
Lawful be it to serve a Trojan spouse;
And Tyrians yield to thy right hand in dower.'
    To whom Venus replied thus, that knew
Her words proceeded from a feigned mind,
To Libyan coasts to turn th' empire from Rome.
' What wight so fond such offer to refuse?
Or yet with thee had liever strive in war?
So be it fortune thy tale bring t' effect:
But destinies I doubt; lest Jove nill grant,

That folk of Tyre, and such as came from Troy,
Should hold one town ; or grant these nations
Mingled to be, or joined aye in league.
Thou art his wife : lawful it is for thee
For to attempt his fancy by request :
Pass on before ; and follow thee I shall.'

  Queen Juno then thus took her tale again :
' This travail be it mine.   But by what mean
(Marke), in few words I shall thee learn eftsoons,
This work in hand may now be compassed.
Æneas now, and wretched Dido eke,
To the forest a hunting mind to wend
To-morn, as soon as Titan shall ascend,
And with his beams hath overspread the world :
And whiles the wings of youth do swarm about,
And whiles they range to overset the groves,
A cloudy shower mingled with hail I shall
Pour down, and then with thunder shake the skies.
Th' assembly scattered the mist shall cloke.
Dido a cave, the Troyan prince the same
Shall enter too ; and I will be at hand :
And if thy will stick unto mine, I shall
In wedlock sure knit, and make her his own :
Thus shall the marriage be.'   To-whose request
Without debate Venus did seem to yield,
And smiled soft, as she that found the wile.

  Then from the seas the dawning gan arise :
The sun once up, the chosen youth gan throng
Out at the gates : the hayes so rarely knit,

The hunting staves with their broad heads of steel;
And of Masile the horsemen forth they brake;
Of scenting hounds a kennel huge likewise.
And at the threshold of her chamber door
The Carthage lords did on the Queen attend.
The trampling steed with gold and purple trapp'd,
Chewing the foamy bit, there fiercely stood.
Then issued she, awaited with great train,
Clad in a cloak of Tyre embroider'd rich.
Her quiver hung behind her back, her tress
Knotted in gold, her purple vesture eke
Button'd with gold.   The Troyans of her train
Before her go, with gladsome Iulus.
Æneas eke, the goodliest of the rout,
Makes one of them, and joineth close the throngs:
Like when Apollo leaveth Lycia,
His wint'ring place, and Xanthus' floods likewise,
To visit Delos, his mother's mansion,
Repairing eft and furnishing her choir:
The Candians, and folks of Driopes,
With painted Agathyrsies shout, and cry,
Environing the altars round about;
When that he walks upon mount Cynthus' top:
His sparkled tress repress'd with garlands soft
Of tender leaves, and trussed up in gold;
His quivering darts clatt'ring behind his back.
So fresh and lusty did Æneas seem;
Such lordly port in present countenance.
    But to the hills and wild holts when they came;

From the rock's top the driven savage rose.
Lo from the hill above on th' other side,   [course.
Through the wide lawns they gan to take their
The harts likewise in troops taking their flight,
Raising the dust, the mountain fast forsake.
The child Iulus, blithe of his swift steed,
Amid the plain now pricks by them, now these;
And to encounter wisheth oft in mind
The foaming boar instead of fearful beasts;
Or Lion brown might from the hill descend.

   In the mean while the skies gan rumble sore;
In tail thereof, a mingled shower with hail.
The Tyrian folk, and eke the Troyans youth,
And Venus' nephew the cottages? for fear
Sought round about; the floods fell from the hills.
Dido a den, the Troyan prince the same,   '
Chanced upon.   Our mother then, the Earth,
And Juno that hath charge of marriage,
First tokens gave with burning gleads of flame;
And, privy to the wedlock, lightning skies;
And the Nymphs yelled from the mountains top.

   Ay me! this was the first day of their mirth,
And of their harms the first occasion eke.
Respect of fame no longer her withholds:
Nor museth now to frame her love by stealth.
Wedlock she calls it: under the pretence
Of which fair name she cloaketh now her fault.

   Forthwith Fame flieth through the great Libyan
    towns: '

A mischief Fame, there is none else so swift;
That moving grows, and flitting gathers force.
First small for dread, soon after climbs the skies;
Stayeth on earth, and hides her head in clouds.
Whom our mother the earth, tempted by wrath
Of Gods, begat; the last Sister (they write)
To Cäeus, and to Enceladus eke:
Speedy of foot, of wing likewise as swift,
A monster huge, and dreadful to descrive.
In every plume that on her body sticks
(A thing indeed much marvelous to hear)
As many waker eyes lurk underneath,
So many mouths to speak, and listening ears.
By night she flies amid the cloudy sky,
Shrieking, by the dark shadow of the earth,
Ne doth decline to the sweet sleep her eyes.
By day she sits to mark on the house top,
Or turrets high; and the great towns affrays;
As mindful of ill and lies, as blasing truth.
     This monster blithe with many a tale gan sow
This rumor then into the common ears:
As well things done, as that was never wrought:
As, that there comen is to Tyrian's court
Æneas, one outsprung of Troyan blood,
To whom fair Dido would herself be wed:
And that, the while, the winter long they pass
In foul delight, forgetting charge of reign;
Led against honour with unhonest lust.
     This in each mouth the filthy Goddess spreads;
                    11

And takes her course to king Hiarbas straight,
Kindling his mind; with tales she feeds his wrath;
Gotten was he by Ammon Jupiter
Upon the ravish'd nymph of Garamant.
A hundred hugy, great temples he built
In his far stretching realms to Jupiter;
Altars as many kept with waking flame,
A watch always upon the Gods to tend;
The floors embru'd with yielded blood of beasts,
And threshold spread with garlands of strange hue.
He woode of mind, kindled by bitter bruit
Tofore th' altars, in presence of the Gods,
With reared hands gan humbly Jove entreat:
　'Almighty God! whom the Moores nation
Fed at rich tables presenteth with wine,
See'st thou these things? or fear we thee in vain,
When thou lettest fly thy thunder from the clouds?
Or do those flames with vain noise us affray?
A woman, that wandering in our coasts hath bought
A plot for price, where she a city set;
To whom we gave the strond for to manure,
And laws to rule her town, our wedlock loathed,
Hath chose Æneas to command her realm.
That Paris now, with his unmanly sort,
With mitred hats, with ointed bush and beard,
His rape enjoyeth: whiles to thy temples we
Our offerings bring, and follow rumours vain.'
　Whom praying in such sort, and griping eke
The altars fast, the mighty father heard;

And writhed his look toward the royal walls,
And lovers eke, forgetting their good name.
To Mercury then gave he thus in charge:
'Hence, son, in haste! and call to thee the winds;
Slide with thy plumes, and tell the Troyan prince
That now in Carthage loitereth, rechless
Of the towns granted him by destiny.
Swift through the skies see thou these words convey:
His fair Mother behight him not to us
Such one to be; ne therefore twice him saved
From Greekish arms: but such a one
As meet might seem great Italy to rule,
Dreadful in arms, charged with seigniory,
Shewing in proof his worthy Teucrian race;
And under laws the whole world to subdue.
If glory of such things nought him enflame,
Ne that he lists seek honour by some'pain;
The towers yet of Rome, being his sire,
Doth he envy to young Ascanius?
What mindeth he to frame? or on what hope
In en'mies land doth he make his abode?
Ne his offspring in Italy regards?
Ne yet the land of Lavine doth behold?
Bid him make sail: have here the sum and end;
Our message thus report.' When Jove had said,
Then Mercury 'gan bend him to obey
His mighty father's will: and to his heels
His golden wings he knits, which him transport,
With a light wind above the earth and seas.

And then with him his wand he took, whereby
He calls from hell pale ghosts; and other some
Thither also he sendeth comfortless:
Whereby he forceth sleeps, and them bereaves;
And mortal eyes he closeth up in death.
By power whereof he drives the winds away,
And passeth eke amid the troubled clouds,
Till in his flight he gan descry the top
And the steep flanks of rocky Atlas' hill,
That with his crown sustains the welkin up:
Whose head forgrown with pine, circled alway
With misty clouds, is beaten with wind and storm;
His shoulders spread with snow; and from his chin
The springs descend; his beard frozen with ice.
Here Mercury with equal shining wings
First touched; and with body headling bet,
To the water then took he his descent:
Like to the fowl that endlong coasts and stronds
Swarming with fish, flies sweeping by the sea;
Cutting betwixt the winds and Libyan lands,
From his grandfather by the mother's side,
Cyllène's child so came, and then alight
Upon the houses with his winged feet;
Tofore the towers where he Æneas saw
Foundations cast, arearing lodges new;
Girt with a sword of jasper, starry bright;
A shining 'parel, flamed with stately eye
Of Tyrian purple, hung his shoulders down,
The gift and work of wealthy Dido's hand,

Striped throughout with a thin thread of gold.

Thus he encounters him: 'Oh careless wight!
Both of thy realm, and of thine own affairs;
A wife-bound man now dost thou rear the walls
Of high Carthage, to build a goodly town!
From the bright skies the ruler of the Gods
Sent me to thee, that with his beck commands
Both heav'n and earth: in haste he gave me charge
Through the light air this message thee to say.
What framest thou? or on what hope thy time
In idleness dost waste in Afric land?
Of so great things if nought the fame thee stir,
Ne list by travail honour to pursue;
Ascanius yet, that waxeth fast, behold;
And the hope of Iulus' seed, thine heir;
To whom the realm of Italy belongs,
And soil of Rome.' When Mercury had said,
Amid his tale far off from mortal eyes
Into light air he vanish'd out of sight.

Æneas with that vision striken down,
Well near distraught, upstart his hair for dread,
Amid his throat al his voice likewise 'gan stick.
For to depart by night he longeth now,
And the sweet land to leave, astoined sore
With this advise and message of the Gods.
What may he do, alas! or by what words
Dare he persuade the raging Queen in love?
Or in what sort may he his tale begin?
Now here, now there his rechless mind 'gan run,

And diversely him draws, discoursing all.
After long doubts this sentence seemed best:
Mnestheus first, and strong Cloanthus eke
He calls to him, with Sergest; unto whom
He gave in charge his navy secretly
For to prepare, and drive to the sea coast
His people; and their armour to address;
And for the cause of change to feign excuse:
And that he, when good Dido least foreknew,
Or did suspect so great a love could break,
Would wait his time to speak thereof most meet;
The nearest way to hasten his intent.
Gladly his will and-biddings they obey.

    Full soon the Queen this crafty sleight 'gan smell,
(Who can deceive a lover in forecast?)
And first foresaw the motions for to come;
Things most assured fearing.   Unto whom
That wicked Fame reported, how to flight
Was arm'd the fleet, all ready to avale.
Then ill bested of counsel, rageth she;
And whisketh through the town: like Bacchus' nun,
As Thyas stirs, the sacred rites begun,
And when the wonted third years sacrifice
Doth prick her forth, hearing Bacchus' name hal-
      lowed,
And that the feastful night of Citheron
Doth call her forth, with noise of dancing.

    At length herself bordeth Æneas thus:
'Unfaithful wight! to cover such a fault

Couldest thou hope? unwist to leave my land?
Not thee our love, nor yet right hand betrothed,
Ne cruel death of Dido may withhold?
But that thou wilt in winter ships prepare,
And try the seas in broil of whirling winds?
What if the land thou seekest were not strange!
If not unknowen? or ancient Troy yet stood?
In rough seas yet should Troye town be sought?
Shunnest thou me?   By these tears, and right hand,
(For nought else have I, wretched, left myself)
By our spousals and marriage begun,
If I of thee deserved ever well,
Or thing of mine were ever to thee lief;
Rue on this realm, whose ruin is at hand.
If ought be left that prayer may avail,
I thee beseech to do away this mind.
The Libyans, and tyrants of Nomadane,
For thee me hate: my Tyrians eke for thee
Are wroth; by thee my shamefastness eke stained,
And good renown, whereby up to the stars
Peerless I clamb.   To whom wilt thou me leave,
Ready to die, my sweet guest? sith this name
Is all, as now, that of a spouse remains.
But whereto now should I prolong my death?
What! until my brother Pigmalion
Beat down my walls? or the Getulian king
Hiarbas, yet captive lead me away?
Before thy flight a child had I once borne,
Or seen a young Æneas in my court

Play up and down, that might present thy face,
All utterly I could not seem forsaken.'
    Thus said the Queen.   He to the God's advice,
Unmoved held his eyes, and in his breast
Represt his care, and strove against his will:
And these few words at last then forth he cast.
' Never shall I deny, Queen, thy desert;
Greater than thou in words may well express.
To think on thee ne irk me aye it shall,
Whiles of myself I shall have memory;
And whiles the spirit these limbs of mine shall rule.
For present purpose somewhat shall I say.
Never meant I to cloak the same by stealth,
Slander me not, ne to escape by flight:
Nor I to thee pretended marriage;
Ne hither came to join me in such league.
If destiny at mine own liberty,
To lead my life would have permitted me,
After my will, my sorrow to redoub,
Troy and the remainder of our folk
Restore I should: and with these scaped hands,
The walls again unto these vanquished,
And palace high of Priam eke repair.
But now Apollo, called Grineus,
And prophecies of Lycia me advise
To seize upon the realm of Italy:
That is my love, my country, and my land.
If Carthage turrets thee, Phœnician born,
And of a Libyan town the sight detain;

To us Troyans why doest thou then envy
In Italy to make our resting seat?
Lawful is eke for us strange realms to seek.
As oft as night doth cloak with shadows dark
The earth, as oft as flaming stars appear,
The troubled ghost of my father Anchises
So oft in sleep doth fray me, and advise:
The wronged head by me of my dear son,
Whom I defraud of the Hesperian crown,
And lands allotted him by destiny.
The messenger eke of the Gods but late
Sent down from Jove (I swear by either head)
Passing the air, did this to me report.
In bright day-light the God myself I saw
Enter these walls, and with these ears him heard.
Leave then with plaint to vex both thee and me:
Against my will to Italy I go.'
    Whiles in this sort he did his tale pronounce,
With wayward look she 'gan him aye behold,
And rolling eyes, that moved to and fro;
With silent look discoursing over all:
And forth in rage at last thus 'gan she upbraid:
    'Faithless! forsworn! ne Goddess was thy dam!
Nor Dardanus beginner of thy race!
But of hard rocks mount Caucase monstruous
Bred thee, and teats of Tyger gave thee suck.
But what should I dissemble now my cheer?
Or me reserve to hope of greater things?
Minds he our tears? or ever moved his eyen?

Wept he for ruth? or pitied he our love?
What shall I set before? or where begin?
Juno, nor Jove with just eyes this beholds.
Faith is no where in surety to be found.
Did I not him, thrown up upon my shore
In need receive, and fonded eke invest
Of half my realm? his navy lost, repair?
From death's danger his fellows eke defend?
Ay me! with rage and furies, lo! I drive.
Apollo now, now Lycian prophecies,
Another while, the messenger of Gods,
He says, sent down from mighty Jove himself.
The dreadful charge amid the skies hath brought.
As though that were the travail of the Gods,
Or such a care their quietness might move!
I hold thee not, nor yet gainsay thy words:
To Italy pass on by help of winds;
And through the floods go search thy kingdom new.
If ruthful Gods have any power, I trust
Amid the rocks thy guerdon thou shalt find;
When thou shalt clepe full oft on Dido's name.
With burial brandes I, absent, shall thee chase:
And when cold death from life these limbs divides,
My ghost each where shall still on thee await.
Thou shalt abye; and I shall hear thereof,
Among the souls below the bruit shall come.'
    With such like words she cut off half her tale,
With pensive heart abandoning the light.
And from his sight herself gan far remove;

Forsaking him, that many things in fear
Imagined, and did prepare to say.
Her swouning limbs her damsels 'gan relieve,
And to her chamber bare of marble stone;
And laid her on her bed with tapets spread.

　But just Æneas, though he did desire
With comfort sweet her sorrows to appease,
And with his words to banish all her care;
Wailing her much, with great love overcome:
The Gods' will yet he worketh, and resorts
Unto his navy.　Where the Troyans fast
Fell to their work, from the shore to unstock
High rigged ships: now fletes the tallowed keel;
Their oars with leaves yet green from wood they
　　　　bring;
And masts unshave for haste, to take their flight.
You might have seen them throng out of the town
Like ants, when they do spoil the bing of corn,
For winter's dread, which they bear to their den:
When the black swarm creeps over all the fields,
And thwart the grass by strait paths drags their prey:
The great grains then some on their shoulders truss,
Some drive the troop, some chastise eke the slow:
That with their travail chafed is each path.

　Beholding this, what thought might Dido have?
What sighs gave she? when from her towers high
The large coasts she saw haunted with Troyan's
　　　　works,
And in her sight the seas with din confounded?

O, witless Love! what thing is that to do
A mortal mind thou canst not force thereto?
Forced she is to tears ay to return,
With new requests to yield her heart to love:
And lest she should before her causeless death
Leave any thing untried: 'O Sister Anne!'
Quoth she, 'behold the whole coast round about,
How they prepare, assembled every where;
The streaming sails abiding but for wind:
The shipmen crown their ships with boughs for joy.
O sister! if so great a sorrow I
Mistrusted had, it were more light to bear.
Yet natheless this for me wretched wight,
Anne, shalt thou do: for faithless, thee alone
He reverenced, thee eke his secrets told;
The meetest time thou knowest to borde the man:
To my proud foe thus, Sister, humbly say;
I with the Greeks within the port Aulide
Conjured not, the Troyans to destroy;
Nor to the walls of Troy yet sent my fleet:
Nor cinders of his father Anchises
Disturbed have, out of his sepulture.
Why lets he not my words sink in his ears
So hard to overtreat?   Whither whirls he?
This last boon yet grant he to wretched love.
Prosperous winds for to depart with ease
Let him abide; the foresaid marriage now,
That he betray'd, I do not him require;
Nor that he should fair Italy forgo:

Neither I would he should his kingdom leave.
Quiet I ask, and a time of delay,
And respite eke my fury to assuage,
Till my mishap teach me, all comfortless,
How for to wail my grief.   This latter grace,
Sister, I crave: have thou remorse of me;
Which, if thou shalt vouchsafe, with heaps I shall
Leave by my death redoubled unto thee.'
    Moisted with tears thus wretched gan she plain:
Which Anne reports, and answer brings again.
Nought tears him move, ne yet to any words
He can be framed with gentle mind to yield.
The Werdes withstand, a God stops his meek ears.
Like to the aged boisteous bodied oak,
The which among the Alps the Northern winds
Blowing now from this quarter, now from that,
Betwixt them strive to overwhelm with blasts:
The whistling air among the branches roars,
Which all at once bow to the earth her crops,
The stock once smit: whiles in the rocks the tree
Sticks fast; and look, how high to the heav'n her top
Rears up, so deep her root spreads down to hell.
So was this Lord now here now there beset
With words; in whose stout breast wrought many
        cares.
But still his mind in one remains; in vain
The tears were shed.   Then Dido, fray'd of Fates,
Wisheth for death, irked to see the skies.
And that she might the rather work her will,

And leave the light, (a grisly thing to tell)
Upon the altars burning full of 'cense
When she set gifts of sacrifice, she saw
The holy water stocks wax black within;
The wine eke shed, change into filthy gore:
This she to none, not to her sister told.
A marble temple in her palace eke,
In memory of her old spouse, there stood,
In great honour and worship, which she held,
With snow white clothes deck'd, and with boughs
    of feast:
Whereout was heard her husband's voice, and speech
Cleping for her, when dark night hid the earth:
And oft the owl with rueful song complain'd
From the housetop, drawing long doleful tunes.
And many things forespoke by prophets past
With dreadful warning 'gan her now affray:
And stern Æneas seemed in her sleep
To chase her still about, distraught in rage:
And still her thought, that she was left alone
Uncompanied, great voyages to wend,
In desert land, her Tyrian folk to seek.
Like Pentheus, that in his madness saw
Swarming in flocks the furies all of hell;
Two suns remove, and Thebès town shew twain.
Or like Orestes Agamemnon's son,
In tragedies who represented aye
Is driven about, that from his mother fled
Armed with brands, and eke with serpent's black;

That sitting found within the temple's porch
The ugly furies his slaughter to revenge.

Yelden to woe, when phrensy had her caught,
Within herself then gan she well debate,
Full bent to die, the time and eke the mean;
And to her woful sister thus she said,
In outward cheer dissembling her intent,
Presenting hope under a semblant glad:

'Sister, rejoice! for I have found the way
Him to return, or loose me from his love.
Toward the end of the great ocean flood,
Whereas the wandering sun descendeth hence,
In the extremes of Ethiope, is a place
Where huge Atlas doth on his shoulders turn
The sphere so round with flaming stars beset.
Born of Massyle, I hear should be a Nun;
That of the Hesperian sisters' temple old,
And of their goodly garden keeper was;
That gives unto the Dragon eke his food,
That on the tree preserves the holy fruit;
That honey moist, and sleeping poppy casts.
This woman doth avaunt, by force of charm,
What heart she list to set at liberty;
And other some to pierce with heavy cares:
In running flood to stop the waters' course;
And eke the stars their movings to reverse;
T' assemble eke the ghosts that walk by night:
Under thy feet the earth thou shalt behold
Tremble and roar; the oaks come from the hill.

The Gods and thee, dear Sister, now I call
In witness, and thy head to me so sweet,
To magic arts against my will I bend.
Right secretly within our inner court,
In open air rear up a stack of wood;
And hang thereon the weapon of this man,
The which he left within my chamber, stick:
His weeds dispoiled all, and bridal bed,
Wherein, alas! Sister, I found my bane,
Charge thereupon; for so the Nun commands,
To do away what did to him belong,
Of that false wight that might remembrance bring.
   Then whisted she; the pale her face gan stain.
Ne could yet Anne believe, her sister meant
To cloke her death by this new sacrifice;
Nor in her breast such fury did conceive:
Neither doth she now dread more grievous thing
Than followed Sichées death; wherefore
She put her will in ure. But then the Queen,
When that the stack of wood was reared up
Under the air within the inward court
With cloven oak, and billets made of fir,
With garlands she doth all beset the place,
And with green boughs eke crown the funeral,
And thereupon his weeds and sword yleft,
And on a bed his picture she bestows,
As she that well foreknew what was to come.
The altars stand about, and eke the Nun
With sparkled tress; the which three hundred Gods

With a loud voice doth thunder out at once,
Erebus the grisly, and Chaos huge,
And eke the threefold Goddess Hecate,
And three faces of Diana the virgin :
And sprinkles eke the water counterfeit
Like unto black Avernus' lake in hell :
And springing herbs reap'd up with brazen scythes
Were sought, after the right course of the Moon ;
The venom black intermingled with milk ;
The lump of flesh 'tween the new born foals eyen
To reave, that winneth from the dam her love.
She, with the mole all in her hands devout,
Stood near the altar, bare of the one foot,
With vesture loose, the bands unlaced all ;
Bent for to die, calls the Gods to record,
And guilty stars eke of her destiny :
And if there were any God that had care
Of lovers' hearts not moved with love alike,
Him she requires of justice to remember.
    It was then night; the sound and quiet sleep
Had through the earth the wearied bodies caught;
The woods, the raging seas were fallen to rest ;
When that the stars had half their course declined ;
The fields whist, beasts, and fowls of divers hue,
And what so that in the broad lakes remained,
Or yet among the bushy thicks of brier,
Laid down to sleep by silence of the night
'Gan swage their cares, mindless of travails past.
Not so the spirit of this Phenician ;
Unhappy she that on no sleep could chance,

Nor yet night's rest enter in eye or breast:
Her cares redouble; love doth rise and rage
    again,
And overflows with swelling storms of wrath.
Thus thinks she then, this rolls she in her mind:
  'What shall I do? shall I now bear the scorn,
For to assay mine old wooers again?
And humbly yet a Numid spouse require,
Whose marriage I have so oft disdained?
The Troyan navy, and Teucrian vile commands
Follow shall I? as though it should avail,
That whilom by my help, they were relieved;
Or for because with kind and mindful folk
Right well doth sit the passed thankful deed?
Who would me suffer (admit this were my will)?
Or me scorned to their proud ships receive?
Oh, woe-begone! full little knowest thou yet
The broken oaths of Laomedon's kind.
What then? alone on merry mariners
Shall I wait? or board them with my power
Of Tyrians assembled me about?
And such as I with travail brought from Tyre
Drive to the seas, and force them sail again?
But rather die, even as thou hast deserved;
And to this woe with iron give thou end.
And thou, Sister, first vanquish'd with my tears,
Thou in my rage with all these mischiefs first
Didst burden me, and yield me to my foe.
Was it not granted me from spousals free,
Like to wild beasts, to live without offence,

Without taste of such cares? is there no faith
Reserved to the cinders of Sychee?'
    Such great complaints brake forth out of her
        breast:
Whiles Æneas full minded to depart,
All things prepared, slept in the poop on high.
To whom in sleep the wonted Godhead's form
Gan aye appear, returning in like shape
As seemed him; and 'gan him thus advise:
Like unto mercury in voice and hue,
With yellow bush, and comely limbs of youth.
'O Goddess son, in such case canst thou sleep?
Ne yet, bestraught, the dangers dost foresee,
That compass thee? nor hear'st the fair winds
        blow?
Dido in mind rolls vengeance and deceit;
Determ'd to die, swells with unstable ire.
Wilt thou not flee whiles thou hast time of flight?
Straight shalt thou see the seas covered with sails,
The blazing brands the shore all spread with flame,
And if the morrow steal upon thee here.
Come off, have done, set all delay aside;
For full of change these women be alway.'
This said, in the dark night he gan him hide.
    Æneas, of this sudden vision
Adread, starts up out of his sleep in haste;
Calls up his feres: 'Awake, get up, my men,
Aboard your ships, and hoise up sail with speed;
A God me wills, sent from above again,
To haste my flight, and wreathen cables cut.

O holy God, what so thou art, we shall
Follow thee, and all blithe obey thy will;
Be at our hand, and friendly us assist;
Address the stars with prosperous influence.'
And with that word his glistering sword unsheaths;
With which drawn he the cables cut in twain.
The like desire the rest embraced all.
All thing in haste they cast, and forth they whirl;
The shores they leave; with ships the seas are
      spread;
Cutting the foam by the blue seas they sweep.
  Aurora now from Titan's purple bed
With new daylight had overspread the earth;
When by her windows the Queen the peeping day
Espied, and navy with 'splay'd sails depart
The shore, and eke the port of vessels void.
Her comely breast thrice or four times she smote
With her own hand, and tore her golden tress.
'Oh Jove,' quoth she, 'shall he then thus depart,
A stranger thus, and scorn our kingdom so?
Shall not my men do on their armour prest,
And eke pursue them throughout all the town?
Out of the road soon shall the vessel warp.
Haste on, cast flame, set sail, and wield your oars.
What said I? but where am I? what phrensy
Alters thy mind?   Unhappy Dido, now
Hath thee beset a froward destiny.
Then it behoved, when thou didst give to him
His sceptre.   Lo! his faith and his right hand!
That leads with him, they say, his country Gods,

That on his back his aged father bore!
His body might I not have caught and rent?
And in the seas drenched him and his feres?
And from Ascanius his life with iron reft,
And set him on his father's board for meat?
Of such debate perchance the fortune might
Have been doubtful: would God it were assay'd!
Whom should I fear, sith I myself must die?
Might I have throwen into that navy brands,
And filled eke their decks with flaming fire,
The father, son, and all their nation
Destroy'd, and fallen myself dead over all!
Sun with thy beams, that mortal works descriest;
And thou, Juno, that well these travails know'st;
Proserpine, thou, upon whom folk do use
To howl, and call in forked ways by night;
Infernal Furies eke, ye wreakers of wrong;
And Dido's Gods, who stands at point of death,
Receive these words, and eke your heavy power
Withdraw from me, that wicked folk deserve:
And our request accept we you beseech:
If so that yonder wicked head must needs
Recover port, and sail to land of force;
And if Jove's will have so resolved it,
And such end set as no wight can foredo;
Yet at the least assailed might he be
With arms and wars of hardy nations;
From the bounds of his kingdom far exiled;
Iulus eke ravish'd out of his arms;
Driven to call for help, that may he see

The guiltless corpses of his folk lie dead :
And after hard conditions of peace,
His realm, nor life desired may he brook ;
But fall before his time, ungraved amid the sands.
This I require ; these words with blood I shed.
And, Tyrians, ye his stock and all his race
Pursue with hate ; reward our cinders so.
No love nor league betwixt our peoples be ;
And of our bones some wreaker may there spring,
With sword and flame that Troyans may pursue :
And from henceforth, when that our power may
        stretch,
Our coasts to them contrary be for aye,
I crave of God ; and our streams to their floods ;
Arms unto arms ; and offspring of each race
With mortal war each other may fordo.'
    This said, her mind she writhed on all sides,
Seeking with speed to end her irksome life.
To Sichees' nurse Barcen then thus she said,
(For hers at home in ashes did remain) :
' Call unto me, dear Nurse, my Sister Anne :
Bid her in haste in water of the flood
She sprinkle the body, and bring the beasts,
And purging sacrifice I did her shew ;
So let her come : and thou thy temples bind
With sacred garlands : for the sacrifice
That I to Pluto have begun, my mind
Is to perform, and give end to these cares ;
And Troyan statue throw into the flame.'
    When she had said, redouble gan her nurse

Her steps, forth on an aged woman's trot.
   But trembling Dido eagerly now bent
Upon her stern determination;
Her bloodshot eyes rolling within her head;
Her quivering cheeks flecked with deadly stain,
Both pale and wan to think on death to come;
Into the inward wards of her palace
She rusheth in, and clamb up, as distraught,
The burial stack, and drew the Troyan sword,
Her gift sometime, but meant to no such use.
Where when she saw his weed, and well knowen bed,
Weeping awhile in study gan she stay,
Fell on the bed, and these last words she said:
   'Sweet spoils, whiles God and destinies it would,
Receive this sprite, and rid me of these cares:
I lived and ran the course fortune did grant;
And under earth my great ghost now shall wend:
A goodly town I built, and saw my walls;
Happy, alas, too happy, if these coasts
The Troyan ships had never touched aye.'
   This said, she laid her mouth close to the bed.
'Why then,' quoth she, 'unwroken shall we die?
But let us die: for this! and in this sort
It liketh us to seek the shadows dark!
And from the seas the cruel Troyan's eyes
Shall well discern this flame; and take with him
Eke these unlucky tokens of my death!'
   As she had said, her damsels might perceive
Her with these words fall pierced on a sword;
The blade embrued, and hands besprent with gore.

The clamour rang unto the palace top;
The bruit ran throughout all th' astonied town:
With wailing great, and women's shrill yelling
The roofs 'gan roar; the air resound with plaint:
As though Carthage, or th' ancient town of Tyre
With press of enter'd enemies swarmed full:
Or when the rage of furious flame doth take
The temples' tops, and mansions eke of men.
   Her sister Anne, spriteless for dread to hear
This fearful stir, with nails gan tear her face;
She smote her breast, and rushed through the rout:
And her dying she clepes thus by her name:
   'Sister, for this with craft did you me bourd?
The stack, the flame, the altars, bred they this?
What shall I first complain, forsaken wight?
Loathest thou in death thy sister's fellowship?
Thou shouldst have call'd me to like destiny;
One woe, one sword, one hour, might end us both.
This funeral stack built I with these hands,
And with this voice cleped our native Gods?
And, cruel, so absentest me from thy death?
Destroy'd thou hast, Sister, both thee and me,
Thy people eke, and princes born of Tyre.
Give here; I shall with water wash her wounds;
And suck with mouth her breath, if ought be left.'
   This said, unto the high degrees she mounted,
Embracing fast her sister now half dead,
With wailful plaint: whom in her lap she laid,
The black swart gore wiping dry with her clothes.
But Dido striveth to lift up again

Her heavy eyen, and hath no power thereto:
Deep in her breast that fixed wound doth gape.
Thrice leaning on her elbow gan she raise
Herself upward; and thrice she overthrew
Upon the bed: ranging with wand'ring eyes
The skies for light, and wept when she it found.
   Almighty Juno having ruth by this
Of her long pains, and eke her lingering death,
From heaven she sent the Goddess Iris down,
The throwing sprite, and jointed limbs to loose.
For that neither by lot of destiny,
Nor yet by kindly death she perished,
But wretchedly before her fatal day,
And kindled with a sudden rage of flame,
Proserpine had not from her head bereft
The golden hair, nor judged her to hell..
The dewy Iris thus with golden wings,
A thousand hues shewing against the Sun,
Amid the skies then did she fly adown
On Dido's head: where as she gan alight,
'This hair,' quod she, 'to Pluto consecrate,
Commanded I reave; and thy spirit unloose
From this body. And when she thus had said,
With her right hand she cut the hair in twain:
And therewithal the kindly heat gan quench,·
And into wind the life forthwith resolve.

The two following poems are given from a very curious MS. of the time of Henry the VIIIth, belonging to the Duke of Devonshire. The greater part of the poems in that MS. have the names, or the initials of their respective authors subscribed. The signatures originally affixed to those here printed have been much effaced. What remains of them, however, is sufficient to lead to some conjecture. The first is subscribed "Finis q^d. W.   t." The second, "Finis q^d. S   e." Respecting the first of these names I apprehend no doubt can be entertained, especially as a large number of the poems in the volume bear Wyatt's signature. That the latter name was designed for Surrey's, I think extremely probable; for his name was generally spelt "Surreye:" and the letter preceding the final "e," though erased in part, seems to have been "y." I believe that many compositions have been ascribed to authors on presumptive evidence less strong than the present. It should be observed, that Surrey and Wyatt were in the habit of frequently communicating their verses to each other. See the poems in this volume, which begin; "As oft as I behold and see;" p. 37: and "Love that liveth and reigneth in my thought;" p. 11. — *Dr. Nott.*

PRIMUS.

My fearful hope from me is fled,
Which of long time hath been my guide.
Now faithful trust is in his stead,
And bids me set all fear aside.
    O' truth it is, I not deny,
All Lovers may not live in ease.

Yet some by hap doth hit truly;
So like may I, if that she please.
   Why! so it is a gift, ye wot,
By nature one to love another.
And since that love doth fall by lot;
Then why not I, as well as other.
   It may so be the cause is why,
She knoweth no part to my poor mind:
But yet as one assuredly
I speak nothing but as I find.
   If Nature will, it shall so be:
No reason ruleth Fantasy.
Yet in this case, as seemeth me,
I take all thing indifferently.
   Yet uncertain I will rejoice,
And think to have, though yet thou hast.
I put my chance unto her choice
With patience, for power is past.
   No! no! I know the like is fair
Without disdain or cruelty:
And so to end from all despair;
Until I find the contrary.

SECUNDUS.

   Your fearful hope cannot prevail;
Nor yet faithful trust also.
Some thinks to hit, ofttimes do fail;
Whereby they change their wealth to woe.

What though! in that yet put no trust:
But always after as ye see.
For say your will, and do your lust;
There is no place for you to be.

No such within; ye are far out.
Your labour lost ye hope to save.
But once I put ye out of doubt;
The thing is had that ye would have.

Though to remain without remorse,
And pitiless to be opprest;
Yet is the course of Love, by force
To take all things unto the best.

Well! yet beware, if thou be wise:
And leave thy hope thy heat to cool:
For fear lest she thy love despise,
Reputing thee but as a fool.

Since this to follow of force thou must,
And by no reason can refrain;
Thy chance shall change thy least mistrust;
As thou shalt prove unto thy pain.

When with such pain thou shalt be paid,
The which shall pass all remedy;
Then think on this that I have said;
And blame thy foolish Fantasy.

FINIS.

INDEX OF FIRST LINES.

ALAS! so all things now do hold their peace, 14.
Although I had a check, 32.
As oft as I behold, and see, 37.
Brittle beauty, that Nature made so frail, 13.
But now the wounded Queen, with heavy care, 153.
Divers thy death do diversely bemoan, 59.
Each beast can choose his fere according to his mind, 47.
From Tuscane came my Lady's worthy race, 12.
From pensive fancies then I gan my heart revoke, 84.
Girt in my guiltless gown, as I sit here and sow, 43.
Give ear to my suit, Lord! fromward hide not thy face, 109.
Give place, ye lovers, here before, 30.
Good ladies! ye that have your pleasure in exile, 27.
If care do cause men cry, why do not I complain, 53.
If he that erst the form so lively drew, 32.
I never saw my Lady lay apart, 16.
In Cyprus springs, whereas dame Venus dwelt, 12.
In the rude age, when knowledge was not rife, 62.
In winter's just return, when Boreas gan his reign, 23.
I, Solomon, David's son, King of Jerusalem, 82.
Laid in my quiet bed, in study as I were, 65.
Like to the steerless boat that swerves with every wind, 89.
London! hast thou accused me, 69.
Love, that liveth and reigneth in my thought, 11.
Martial, the things that do attain, 57.
My Ratclif, when thy rechless youth offends, 68.
My fearful hope from me is fled, 186.
Norfolk sprung thee, Lambeth holds thee dead, 62.
Of thy Life, Thomas, this compass well mark, 58.
O happy dames that may embrace, 21.

O loathsome place! where I, 35.

O Lord! upon whose will dependeth my welfare, 101.

Set me whereas the sun doth parch the green, 15.

Since fortune's wrath envieth the wealth, 46.

So cruel prison how could betide, alas, 17.

Such wayward ways hath Love, that most part in discord, 5.

The sun hath twice brought forth his tender green, 1.

Th' Assyrian king, in peace, with foul desire, 64.

The soote season, that bud and bloom forth brings, 3.

The golden gift that Nature did thee give, 16.

The great Macedon, that out of Persia chased, 59.

The storms are past; the clouds are overblown, 67.

The fancy which that I have served long, 68.

The Sun, when he hath spread his rays, 71.

The sudden storms that heave me to and fro, 104.

They whisted all, with fixed face attent, 115.

Though I regarded not, 39.

Though, Lord, to Israel thy graces plenteous be, 105.

Thy name, O Lord, how great, is found before our sight, 111.

Too dearly had I bought my green and youthful years, 34.

When youth had led me half the race, 4.

When Summer took in hand the Winter to assail, 8.

When Windsor walls sustain'd my wearied arm, 14.

When raging love with extreme pain, 20.

When I bethought me well, under the restless Sun, 93.

When that repentant tears hath cleansed clear from ill, 96.

Where rechless youth in an unquiet breast, 101.

Wrapt in my careless cloak, as I walk to and fro, 41.

Wyatt resteth here, that quick could never rest, 60.

Your fearful hope cannot prevail, 187.

THE END.

CPSIA information can be obtained
at www.ICGtesting.com
Printed in the USA
LVHW080959200920
666571LV00008B/38